Referendums and Ethnic Conflict

National and Ethnic Conflict in the Twenty-First Century

Brendan O'Leary, Series Editor

A complete list of books in the series is available from the publisher.

Referendums and Ethnic Conflict

Matt Qvortrup

PENN

UNIVERSITY OF PENNSYLVANIA PRESS

PHILADELPHIA

Published by
University of Pennsylvania Press
Philadelphia, Pennsylvania 19104-4112
www.upenn.edu/pennpress

Printed in the United States of America on acid-free paper
10 9 8 7 6 5 4 3 2 1

Library of Congress Cataloging-in-Publication Data

Qvortrup, Matt.
    Referendums and ethnic conflict / Matt Qvortrup.
        pages cm.— (National and ethnic conflict in the twenty-first century)
    Includes bibliographical references and index.
    ISBN 978-0-8122-4580-6 (hardcover : alk. paper)
    1. Referendum.   2. Ethnic conflict—Political aspects.   3. Ethnic conflict—
Government policy.   I. Title.
JF491.Q95   2014
328.2'3—dc23
                                                                2013038046

The existence of a nation is a daily plebiscite.
—Ernest Renan, *Qu'est-ce qu'une nation?*

Lex est quod populus iubet atque constituit.
—Gaius, *Institutiones*

The History of the world is not the theatre of happiness. Periods of happiness are blank pages in it, for they are periods of harmony,—periods when the antithesis is in abeyance.
—G. W. F. Hegel, *The Philosophy of History*

A Citizen in general is someone who is capable of being a ruler and a subject.
—Aristotle, *Politics*

Contents

Introduction

The core problem in political theory is that fundamental and equally axiomatic principles often collide. A paradox can almost be defined as a clash of two equally incontestable maxims of truth. Two such "truths" are (1) that each nation has a right to determine its own affairs and (2) that the majority has a right to govern. Admittedly these "rights" are tempered by the recognition that no nation and no majority may ride roughshod over minorities. But this caveat notwithstanding, national self-determination and majority rule are principles to which few fundamentally object. Indeed, defending the reverse positions would appear politically absurd. But the problem is that the two principles often are incompatible. To understand why, it might be useful to consider a distinction used in ancient Greek. The Greeks make a distinction between the people as a nation (*ethnos*) and the people as a body of citizens (*demos*).[1] In the classical city-state—or *polis*—the two were congruent, and in some present-day nation-states, such as Norway and Luxembourg, the same is broadly true. But more often than not, the two concepts are in conflict. To take an example, small-town English politician, the Conservative councilor Rob McKella from Corby in Northamptonshire, believes that people in England should be given a right to vote on Scottish independence.[2] After all, he argues, the voters are citizens in the United Kingdom and collectively constitute the demos. However, most people in Scotland, by contrast, believe that only people living north of the border should be allowed to vote as these people—perhaps alongside Scots living in the diaspora—constitute the ethnos and hence have a right to self-determination. As will come to be obvious, these two worldviews, both based on solid arguments, do not combine.

This book is about this conflict between the ethnos and the demos, and about the problems that are raised when solutions to ethnic and national issues and conflicts are sought through referendums. Our main focus is to determine when different kinds and types of referendums on ethnonational issues occur and also to determine if they lead to exacerbation of conflict or the opposite—if balloting can stop bullets.

Referendums have often been perceived to be incompatible with nationalism. William Sumner Maine—a conservative writer from the end of the Victorian age—once mused that "democracies are quite paralyzed by the plea of nationality. There is no more effective way of attacking them than by admitting the right of the majority to govern, but denying that the majority so entitled is the particular majority which claims the right" (Maine 1897: 88).

This book looks at these conflicts through a comprehensive study of all the referendums held on ethnic and nationalist issues from the French Revolution to the 2012 referendum on statehood for Puerto Rico.

It's a controversial topic. Some scholars have supported these referendums on the basis of philosophical conviction and because they believe that they confer legitimacy upon decisions made by elites. Jürgen Habermas, for example, took this view. In light of resentment following new boundaries after the Cold War he found that referendums on sovereignty issues—given certain safeguards—could be "a way of proceeding which permitted a broader discussion *and* opinion formation as well as a more extensive—and, above all, better prepared—participation," which would give the voters "the eventual responsibility for the process" (Habermas 1996: 12). If the people were given the responsibility through referendums they would not be able to complain later on, as "it would have been the people's own mistake that they would have had to cope with" (Habermas 1996: 12). These issues are interesting and important from a philosophical point of view, but they are ultimately issues for political theory and not the primary concern of the comparative and empirical political scientist. Hence these normative issues are not the focus of this study. The questions we look at are *positive* issues of when and why referendums on various national and ethnic issues occur.

These polls have played an important role in attempts to resolve ethnic conflicts for centuries. But it is fair to say that scholars of ethnic and national conflict—as well as political scientists—have had reservations about these plebiscites and referendums. Michael Gallagher, writing about the experience in Europe, concluded that "the referendum is least useful if applied to an issue that runs along the lines of a major cleavage in society" (Gallagher 1996: 246), and recently Jonathan Wheatley wrote about the "disruptive potential of direct democracy in deeply divided societies" (Wheatley 2012: 64). While critical, Wheatley was not as dismissive of referendums as Roger Mac Ginty, who noted, "The principal problem with referendums in situations of profound ethnic conflict is that they are zero-sum, creating winners and losers. Simple majoritarian devices do little to help manage the complexity of conflict. Instead they validate the position of one side and reject that of another. Often, they do little other than delimit and quantify division" (Mac Ginty 2003: 3).

This interpretation may have been correct in the case of the 1973 Border Poll in Northern Ireland (Osborne 1982: 154) and, indeed, in the case of many of the referendums held in former Yugoslavia in the 1990s (Terret 2000). But Mac Ginty's conclusion that "the blunt reductionism of a referendum (for example the perception that a conflict is about a line on a map and little else)" (Mac Ginty 2003, 3) is perhaps a little bit cavalier and perhaps ignores the fact that the Schleswigian conflict, which caused two wars between Denmark and Germany, was resolved by a referendum (Laponce 2010 24). Indeed, Sarah Wambaugh noted in her much-quoted study *Plebiscites Since the World War* that "the plebiscite was so fair and excellently administered that the Schleswig question, which caused three wars in the 19th Century and rent of councils of Europe for some seventy years, has ceased to exist" (Wambaugh 1933: 98).

A referendum is admittedly unlikely to work on its own, and referendums have been followed by violence (the case of East Timor in 1999 comes to mind). But this does not prove that the referendum is to blame. Indeed, there are examples of the opposite, including the peaceful poll in Eritrea in 1993 (on secession from Ethiopia).

Just as we can find contrasting empirical examples, we can also find contrasting academic assessments. Some, such as Ben Reilly, maintain that "despite hollow claims that the 'will of the people' must prevail, it is only the most obtuse interpretation that could recommend building peace this way" (Reilly 2003: 174), while others, notably Arend Lijphart, take the view that "the potential of calling the referendum . . . is a strong stimulus for the majority to be heedful of minority views" (Lijphart 1999: 231).

We have a welter of empirical evidence, but so far there have been no systematic study, no developing of hypotheses, and no general theories. One of the aims of this book is to alter this state of affairs. It is surprising that this task has not been undertaken before. The ethnonational referendum has been around for a long time, and it is still popular. From the Swiss referendum on independence and Bonaparte's France in 1802 (and before that Avignon's incorporation into France in 1791) to more recent referendums on power sharing in Northern Ireland in 1998, autonomy for East Timor in 1999, and statehood for Puerto Rico in 2012, voters have been called upon to decide ethnic issues. There have been more than two hundred of these referendums, and their outcomes have decided the fates of people and peoples from Malta to Micronesia and from Mongolia and Montenegro to Montreal. Some have been held in despotic—and indeed totalitarian—regimes (like the Anschluss Referendum in 1938 in Austria), others have been held in countries with impeccable democratic records such as Switzerland (Jura), Denmark (Greenland), and Canada (Nunavut). This geographical spread and the fact that the same institution has been used across different countries and by very different types of regimes make these referendums both puzzling and challenging.

Although they are never far from the media news stream, these referendums or plebiscites (I use the words interchangeably) have rarely received systematic treatment.[3] Mentioned in passing in one of my previous books (Qvortrup 2003) and in Larry LeDuc's *The Politics of Direct Democracy* (2003), as an aside in David Altman's *Direct Democracy Worldwide* (2011), as an afterthought in Markku Suksi's *Bringing in the People* (1994), and in sections of Rouke, Hiskes, and Zirakzadeh's *Direct Democracy and International Politics* (1992), referendums on national issues and ethnic conflict have been relatively marginalized in scholarly research. The only existing monographs on the subject are Lawrence T. Farley's fairly empirical and theory-free *Plebiscites and Sovereignty* (1986) and, much earlier, Sarah Wambaugh's *Plebiscites Since the World War* (1933). Before that Johannes Mattern's doctoral thesis, *The Employment of the Plebiscite in the Determination of Sovereignty* (1921), dealt with some legal and historical aspects of plebiscites on national self-determination and related issues. At the time when my book was all but finished, Jean Laponce's *Le Référendum de souveraineté: Comparaisons* was published in French (2010). While Professor Laponce's book deals with some of the same issues, my book differs in taking a more *positivist* approach that is more devoted to testing hypotheses and finding general and statistical patterns, whereas *Le Référendum de souveraineté* is a more descriptive study in the very best sense of this word. The two books therefore are complements rather than competitors. I hope that my book will spur other scholars on to consider these issues and that it will be superseded by works that further elaborate on a theme that has received too little treatment before.

Methodology and Testing of Hypotheses

Social scientists have always been strangely fascinated by the exact sciences—though they have not always practiced what they have preached.[4] Ever since at least Thomas Hobbes's *Leviathan* and Baruch Spinoza's *Ethics* it has frequently been the ambition of political and philosophical writers to analyze public affairs with the stringency of Euclidian geometry or, to paraphrase Spinoza's *Ethics*, to conduct political science in the manner of *política more geometrico demonstrate.*[5]

The Competition Proximity Model of Ethnonational Referendums

In recent years in particular it has become *de rigueur* to develop formal models to present theoretical arguments, which subsequently can be tested empirically (Aldrich, Alt, and Lupia 2010), and this tendency has begun to influence scholars specializing in direct democracy (e.g., Setälä 1999). However, neither Hobbes nor Spinoza slavishly followed the razor-sharp logic of strict deductive reasoning. The geometric method that they both espoused provided "mathematical illustrations" rather than proofs in the Euclidian sense (Jesseph 1993). This book does the same. Formal models are proposed and even subjected to quantitative tests. But the statistical arguments do not stand alone. Throughout the book numerical data are contrasted and complemented by case studies and historical narratives. Together they provide a mosaic that point toward general tendencies and trends. The conclusions drawn in the study are inspired by and seen through the prism of formal models; however, the truthfulness of these is determined *not* solely by statistical data but also by circumstantial and even anecdotal evidence. This approach may appear defeatist to the positivist purist, but to the realist living in the practical world of politics the departure from pure mathematical models is justified by the greater ability to draw general conclusions. These caveats notwithstanding, this book loosely follows the positivist approach by proposing that the decision to hold referendums on ethnic and national issues can be explained by a formal model that sees the likelihood (probability) of a referendum being held as result of an inverse relationship between political competition and support for the proposed policy among the constituents. The formal model looks as follows:

$$P_{\text{ref}} = \sum_{i=1}^{n} \frac{C}{(I_m - P_i)^2}$$

According to this *competition proximity model*, the probability, P_{ref} that an actor, i, will submit a national or ethnic issue to a referendum depends on the relationship between the competition, C, the actor is facing, and the squared distance between the actor's preference point P_i, and the preference point of the median voter I_m. If an actor is facing considerable competition (large value for C), and if the actor's preferred policy is a popular one (the value of $[I_m - P_i]^2$ is small), then holding a referendum—especially if this is opposed by his competitors—is likely to give the initiator a boost and strengthen his or her legitimacy.

The bold hypothesis in this book is that most referendums on ethnic and national issues are held as a result of the logic underlying this model. In other words, if the value for C is large (something that, admittedly, is difficult to measure), and if the preferred policy is a popular one (the value of $(I_m - P_i)^2$ is small), then the probability of a referendum will be larger than 1. Formally speaking, referendums on ethnic and national issues (and European integration) are likely to be held if the conditions of the competition proximity model are met.

Of course, this model does not—and cannot—stand alone and throughout will be contrasted with other hypotheses. We shall return to these shortly, but before even starting the analysis it is useful to outline the methodological considerations underlying this study.

The Scientific Method for the Social Sciences

At the most basic level, academic or scholarly research differs from other endeavors because of its method and as a result of the more stringent criteria applied. Scholarly research requires at the most basic that we have:

1. clear definitions of the concepts we are studying;
2. criteria for when we can make firm conclusions; and
3. considerations of when we can compare different instances and facts

In this section I set out to answer these questions in an operational way with a view to addressing the questions in this book. This introduction is not intended to provide an analysis of the more philosophical issues pertaining to social science analysis. It is merely intended to provide an overview and a statement of the methodology that I accept a priori.

"The ultimate goal of a positive science is the development of a 'theory' or, 'hypothesis' that yields valid and meaningful (i.e., not truistic) predictions about phenomena not yet observed," wrote Milton Friedman in "The Methodology of Positive Economics."[6] Developing theories that yield "predictions about phenomena not yet observed" means, in this case, to foresee conditions under which the different kinds of ethnonationalist referendums are likely to occur. For the present purposes we take Karl Popper's falsificationist theory as our point of departure.[7]

Karl Popper's argument is based on simple propositional logic. In his early study *Logik der Forschung* (later published in English as *The Logic of Scientific Discovery* in 1959), Popper challenged the view espoused by the Vienna Circle, namely that scientific statements must obey two conditions: (1) have semantic reference and (2) be of a so-called *modus ponens* form. That is—formally speaking—they must be of the form "If p then q, p, therefore q."

However, as Popper pointed out—with reference to Hume—while statements should have semantic reference, they should be of *modus tollens* form, that is, be of the form "If p then q, not q, then not p." Popper further stressed that the antecedent should be a universal statement (i.e., "*all x are y*") and the consequent should be a singular statement (e.g., of the form "this x is y").

We can explain this by a practical example from political science, namely Duverger's Law (Duverger 1972: 23).[8] The argument, developed by the French political scientist Maurice Duverger, can be summed up as follows:

All countries that have first-past-the-post (FPTPT) systems have two-party systems.

Canada (which uses FPTP) does *not* have a two-party system.

Not all countries that use FPTP have two-party systems.

This hypothesis is true for many countries, such as the United States, Jamaica, Botswana, and so on. But there are cases that break the "law." Now the problem with this statement is that it *stricto sensu* should be considered as falsified, as a first-past-the-post country like the aforementioned

---

*Box 1. Formal Example of Hypothetical Syllogism
and Auxiliary Hypothesis*

Under normal circumstances the formula for testing hypotheses is a *modus tolendo tollens*. It can formally be stated as follows:

$$P \rightarrow Q$$
$$\underline{-Q}$$
$$\underline{-P}$$

With the addition of an auxiliary hypothesis (where R denotes the auxiliary hypotheses), we get

$$P \; (\&R) \rightarrow Q$$
$$\underline{-Q}$$
$$-P \; (\&R)$$

Source: Based on Popper (1963).

Canada—to take but one example (India is another one)—has a multiparty system.

Clearly there is something to Duverger's Law, but a couple of exceptions exist. What do we do? To proceed one might invoke auxiliary hypotheses. One might thus restate the theory thus: countries with FPTP electoral systems *and without* strong regionally based political movements have two-party systems. However, to use such auxiliary hypotheses we must require that such caveats are universal and not ad hoc. Thus, the existence of a particular (nonuniversal) factor—such as, for example, Quebecois nationalism—will not be regarded as acceptable as we are striving for universal laws. In other words, and to quote a scholar from another field, "An auxiliary hypothesis ought to be testable independently of the particular problem it is introduced to solve, independently of the theory it is designed to save (e.g. the evidence for the existence of Neptune is independent of the anomalies in Uranus's orbit)" (Kitcher 1982: 46).

Moreover, we need to add that we should not simply reject a theory once one single case falsifies it and such an approach is—moreover—not consistent with Popper's original formulation of the theory of falsification. It is beyond the scope of this book to delve deeply into the finer points of the theories of science. Suffice it to say that Popper, in his *Logic of Scientific*

Discovery, actually stresses that a theory should be superseded by a rival theory *only if* the new theory can explain the things the former theory could explain as well as the things it could not explain (Popper 1959: 57).

But doing this alone does not solve the problem. Often in political science we are faced with a rather simplistic approach to causal inference. We assume a generality, and then proceed to prove it. Popper notwithstanding, we are typically dealing with statements of the form "If p then q, p therefore q" (or, formally speaking, what logicians call a *modus ponens*).

This form of statement will be transformed into hypotheses based on the competition proximity model (see page 6) and tested statistically. However, there is no suggestion that merely a high r^2 and high levels of statistical significance are sufficient to render the model plausible. While some analyses of the policy effects of electoral systems may have suggested this (Lijphart 1999), it is rarely the case that there is a direct, quantifiable, and causal relationship between variables. A high r^2 may indicate an underlying causal relation, but the explanation is key. For example, it is possible that there is a correlation between the number of referendums and a particular system's degree of democratization (e.g., as measured by the Freedom House scores),[9] but this does not in itself imply or indicate that there is a causal relationship between referendums and dictatorship. Rather this seeming correlation might be a result of intervening and far more important, and indeed interesting, variables. For example, it has been argued that there is a correlation between economic growth and first-past-the-post electoral systems. This is not, however, because this electoral system in itself leads to growth, but more likely a result of an intervening variable, namely that single-party governments (which are more common in countries with first-past-the-post systems) are less likely to negotiate costly deals with minority parties (Marsiliani and Renström 2007), which in turn would have reduced the funds available for investment.

Finding these regularities, however, is not just about conducting large comparative studies across dozens of cases. To fully understand the logic of the regularities (if they exist) also requires us to probe into particular examples. For, to quote a prominent American comparativist, "If statistics address questions of propensities, narratives address questions of process" (Laitin 2002: 247). Or put differently, an understanding of the "laws" is aided by case studies that explain the mechanics of the causal relationships.

Hence, in addition to the theoretically based analysis, the book also contains descriptive, yet analytical, case studies. These cases studies will also help us to find special circumstances that explain anomalies. This is sometimes a complex business and suffers from the fact that we sometimes have to "feel" our way into a problem. This more qualitative addendum to the more formal analysis has been summed up as the process of "sociological imagination," namely "the capacity to shift from one perspective to another—from the political to the psychological; from examination of a single family to comparative assessment of the national budgets of the world; from the theological school to the military establishment; from considerations of an oil industry to studies of contemporary poetry" (Mills 1951: 11). Getting this right is a tricky business, and there is no guarantee that we get it right even though we follow the logic.

A Typology of Ethnonational Referendums

These methodological rules are the bare bones of the analysis. But ethnonational referendums are not a uniform category. The referendum on devolution in Wales in March 2011 was vastly different from the referendum held on independence in South Sudan a few months before. Similarly, the referendum held in the Soviet Union in March 1991 was vastly different from the vote held in Saarland between Germany and France in 1955. In other words, the category "ethnonational referendums" is so broad that it might be meaningless. To paraphrase Aaron Wildavsky, if ethno national referendums are everything then maybe they are nothing (Wildavsky 1973). What we need is a set of more precise definitions, which can subsequently form part of testable hypotheses.

Social science is—or ought to be—a cumulative endeavor. The research developed by scholars provides the basis for the research undertaken by a subsequent generation. Furthermore, research in a subarea is often based on a larger framework developed for more general problems. This model is generally inspired by and based upon the taxonomy developed by Brendan O'Leary and John McGarry, who distinguish between, respectively, "difference-managing policies" and "difference-eliminating policies" (see, e.g., McGarry and O'Leary 1993; updated in O'Leary2001a). Using O'Leary and McGarry's definition we can thus have referendums on

1. Difference elimination, that is, referendums that aim at legitimizing a policy of homogenization, such as the Anschluss referendum in Austria in 1938

Table 1. Typology of Ethnonational Referendums

International/homogenizing	International heterogenizing
Secession referendums	Right-sizing referendums
Example: Eritrea 1993	Example: Schleswig referendums 1920
National homogenizing	**National heterogenizing**
Difference-eliminating referendums	Difference-managing referendums
Example: Egypt and Syria 1958	Example: Wales 2011

2. Difference managing, that is, referendums aimed at managing ethnic or national differences, such as the referendums on devolution in Scotland, Wales, and Northern Ireland in 1997 and 1998

Yet, in order to be more specific, this model is expanded by two categories. In addition to O'Leary and McGarry's taxonomy, we thus expand our model to include

3. Secession referendums, that is, plebiscites to endorse (or otherwise) a territory's secession from a larger entity (e.g., the referendum in Jamaica in 1963 or the referendum in Eritrea in 1991)
4. Right-sizing referendums, that is, votes dealing with the drawing of disputed borders between countries, such as the border between Croatia and Slovenia, which was the subject of a referendum in 2010

This model can also be stated in a more logical way, namely by developing a typology of different types of ethnonational referendums. Broadly speaking, we can distinguish between referendums that are initiated by politicians who take diversity as an accepted fact and want to manage these differences and, on the other hand, referendums initiated by politicians who do not accept diversity. The former may be categorized as "homogenizing" referendums. The latter may be categorized as "heterogenizing." Homogenizing referendums can be divided into "international" and "national," and the same is true for "heterogenizing" referendums. Doing this we get a two-by-two model of four logically possible types of ethnonational referendums (Table 1).

For example, heterogenic referendums can be either right-sizing referendums (international and heterogenizing), for example the Saar plebiscite in 1955, or they can be internal, that is, held within a single state, for example the referendum on the future of Greenland in 2009 and the referendum in Wales in 2011. Homogenizing referendums can similarly be divided into *internally* held plebiscites (such as the poll in the Soviet Union in 1990 on maintaining Moscow control) (Sheehy 1991) and international homogenizing votes that create a new homogeneous entity, for example, a new monoethnic state, as was the case in Norway in 1905.

Of course, there may be referendums that do not fit into this neat categorization. We should always be mindful of social anthropologist Gregory Bateson's observation in *Steps to an Ecology of Mind* that there is a difference between the "maps" and the "landscape," that is, that the theories are the maps and not the landscape (Bateson 1962: 459). Categorizations are preludes to theories, but are only social constructs that serve as heuristic tools, that enable us to get a better overview of the empirical world. A group of referendums that do not fit the categories are the votes on EU integration and membership. These could be seen as marginal examples of difference-managing referendums, but it is not an easy fit, and hence they will be treated separately; again, the theories are the maps not the landscape, and we are more interested in understanding the latter than in drawing up the former.

The aim of this book is to determine when these different kinds of referendums occur. Overall we propose that referendums on ethnic and national issues are most likely to occur when the conditions of the competition proximity model are met, i.e.,

$$P_{ref} = \sum_{i=1}^{n} \frac{C}{(I_m - P_i)^2}$$

But this model does not and cannot stand alone. In addition to testing the competition proximity model we develop other testable propositions. The hypotheses are the following:

1. Secession/partition referendums tend to occur following the lifting of a long-standing imperial hegemony—but only if there is a broad-based elite commitment to polyarchic government in the country in question (as was the case in the former Soviet republics of Estonia, Latvia, and Lithuania).

2. Right-sizing referendums tend to occur in the wake of a major conflict or in the wake of a regime change, such as in the case of the referendums on border demarcation in the wake of World War I.
3. Difference-eliminating referendums tend to occur in authoritarian regimes, to lend legitimacy to a policy of ethnic and national homogenization, such as in the case of the referendums organized by Mikhail Gorbachev in 1990 and in the case of the 1958 referendum in Egypt-Syria on an amalgamated state.
4. Difference-managing referendums tend to occur in countries with high Freedom House scores, especially following long-standing ethnic disagreement (as in the cases of the Canadian Charlottetown referendum 1992, the 1998 Good Friday referendum in Northern Ireland, and the referendums on Greenland in 1980 and 2010).

In addition to these hypotheses, we surmise that ethnonational referendums tend to result in peaceful resolutions of conflicts only if two conditions are met: (1) elite consensus for the proposed solution and (2) international backing of (or not outright opposition to) the referendum.

Chapter Overview

In Chapter 1 ("The History and Logic of Ethnonational Referendums, 1791–1945") we look at the history of ethnonational referendums up to World War II in light of the competition proximity model. The birth of democratic politics in the modern sense of the word coincided with the emergence of the ideology of nationalism.[10] It is not surprising, therefore, that referendums aimed at resolving ethnic tensions have a long history. Some of the first exercises of democratic involvement were referendums on self-determination held in the aftermath of the French Revolution. The first chapter presents a history from the Napoleonic referendums at the beginning of the nineteenth century through the plebiscites that legitimized the Italian Risorgimento in the 1860s and the referendums on national self-determination in the wake of World War I.

Chapter 2 deals with referendums on difference management. Often referendums are used to approve policies that manage differences. In this chapter, we analyze referendums on the relations between center and periphery in federal states (e.g., the 1992 referendum in Canada). We also examine polls in quasi-federal states (e.g., the referendums on Scottish and Welsh devolution in 1997 and the Welsh referendum in 2011). But difference-managing referendums do not just pertain to territorial differences. The referendums on power sharing in places as different as Northern Ireland (1998) and Burundi (2005) are examples of plebiscites held to add legitimacy to policies of (ethnic) difference management. Why were these polls held? When do governments feel there is a need to get the voters' seal of approval for policies of difference management? Using a large-N analysis and selected case studies, the chapter seeks to establish a general pattern of difference-managing referendum occurrence and relate these to the competition proximity model. In addition to analyzing the genesis of these referendums, the chapter also outlines a model that explains what determines the outcome of these referendums in democratic countries.

In Chapter 3, "Secession and Partition," we look at "political divorce settlements." These were the first referendums to be called by this name and were concerned with secession and partitions. Since then scores of referendums have been held on whether territories should secede. Sometimes these have resulted in peaceful resolutions of long-standing conflicts (e.g., in the case of Norway in 1905, where a referendum was held on secession following negotiations between Norway and the Norwegians' Swedish overlords). But more often than not, these polls have resulted in exacerbated conflicts and deepening of tensions (as was the case in Bosnia-Herzegovina and East Timor). Drawing on the literature on secessions, this chapter uses case studies from the Faroe Islands in 1946 and South Sudan in 2011 to analyze when referendums on secessions and partitions can resolve issues. The chapter also looks at the conditions for using referendums to resolve conflicts peacefully. This chapter is followed by a chapter on the legality of referendums in constitutional law. Often it is believed that a local or state government is simply entitled to hold a referendum on independence without further ado, but—as the chapter shows—this is, legally speaking, rarely the case.

Right-sizing referendums, typically referendums on the drawing of borders between countries that have irredentist populations in neighboring countries, such as Poles in Germany in the aftermath of World War I, are dealt with in Chapter 5. Chapter 6 considers referendums to promote homogenization (difference-eliminating referendums). Whether they are conducted in democratic or nondemocratic regimes, these plebiscites are held to secure the legitimacy of controversial policies. In divided societies, referendums are often held to approve policies aimed at assimilating and integrating groups. Using various regression models and selected case studies, the chapter seeks to establish a general pattern of difference-eliminating referendum occurrence. The chapter also includes a theoretical section on the justification for difference-eliminating referendums as outlined by the controversial German scholar Carl Schmitt. Chapter 7 analyzes referendums on European integration. In Chapter 8 we consider the regulation of ethnonational referendums, through a comparative overview of matters such as the registration of voters, the role of the electoral commission, campaign spending, and broadcasting of campaign material. This chapter also addresses issues such as Who is eligible to vote? Who counts the votes? Who formulates the question? and Should there be a special majority quorum? The book concludes with a summary of the law-like regularities found in the chapters.

Last, a note on the data. There have been many referendums on ethnic and national issues. This book is—unless otherwise stated—based on the data set developed by Laponce (2010), though it has been expanded to include some of the cases in Mattern's doctoral thesis (1921). In addition, I have added referendums on European integration based on Hobolt (2009).

Chapter 1

The History and Logic of Ethnonational Referendums, 1791–1945

> Self-determination and democracy went hand in hand. Self-
> determination might indeed be regarded as implicit in the idea of
> democracy; [if] every man's right is recognised to be consulted about
> the affairs of the political unit to which he belongs, he may be
> assumed to have an equal right to be consulted about the form and
> extent of the unit.
> —E. H. Carr (1942: 39)

Before the French and American Revolutions it was accepted that the ruler had a mandate from God. In fact, in the libretto of Mozart's *The Magic Flute*, first performed in 1791 but originally penned in 1774, the protagonist Sarastro eulogized the divine rights of kings: "The Earth a heavenly kingdom, and mortals like the gods."

But time was running out for this idea. When Avignon (then one of the papal territories) voted to join Republican France in a referendum in 1791, the pope complained—through his emissary—that the consequences of the vote would be that "henceforth everybody [would be able] to choose a new master in accordance with one's pleasure" (Cardinal Rezzonico, quoted in Felix Freudenthal 1891: 3–4); this view the pontiff, with his a priori acceptance of the doctrine of *rex dei gratia*, found plainly "absurd" (Freudenthal 1891: 44).

By the time the pope expressed this opinion his views already had an obsolete ring to them. After 1776, and still more after 1789, it became the unquestioned axiom in politics—whether in autocracies or polyarchic states—that the support of the people, or the "consent of the governed," as it was called in the U.S. Declaration of Independence, was the gold standard of political legitimacy. As Johannes Maltern put it in a classic study,

> The French Revolution proclaimed the dogma that we now term self-determination. . . . The mental and logical process was simple. The people *are* the state *and* the nation; the people are sovereign. As such they have the right to decide, as the ultimate ratio, by popular vote and simple majority, all matters affecting the state and the nation. A people held by force and against their own will within the boundaries and under the sovereignty of any state are not in reality part of that state. They have, consequently, the right to declare their separation from the dominant state and proclaim their independence. (Maltern 1921: 77)

But the interesting question is how this affected the rulers. The answer is, perhaps, that the "dogma" of self-determination became an "informal institution" in the sense that it was—to use North's definition—a "humanly devised constraint that [structures] political . . . interaction" (North 1991: 97). Due to the acceptance of this "informal institution" of the "will of the people," it became necessary for rulers to show that they heeded the wills of the majority of the people; they were institutionally constrained by what we, following James March and Johan P. Olsen, may call "the logic of appropriateness" (March and Olsen 1984:1). This meant that even regimes that were far from free or democratic (in the present-day sense of the word) had to find a way of showing that they were supported by the people and that they legitimately could claim to act in the name of the nation. Of course, the decision to heed the will of the people also had elements of the "logic of consequentiality" to it; ignore the preferences of the demos and the ethnos and you will suffer the consequences. Politics is rarely an altruistic endeavor.

As already noted in the introduction, this overall logic can be summed up formally. Taken as a whole an actor, i, is likely to benefit from a referendum if there is considerable competition, C, and if the squared distance between the actor's preference point and the preference point of the median voter is small. Hence the probability of holding a referendum can be stated as follows:

$$P_{\text{ref}} = \sum_{i=1}^{n} \frac{C}{(I_m - P_i)^2}$$

For example, in 1992 the French president, François Mitterrand, was facing stiff political competition from the far right Front National as well as from the moderate right Rassemblement pour la République (RPR). He perceived—wrongly it turned out—that the distance between his preference point and the preference point of the median voter was minimal; $(P_i - I_m)^2$ was small, and the electoral competition, here denoted as C, was large. The utility of calling a referendum was perceived to be considerable; he could show that he was willing to heed the demands of the people, that he was in touch. Hence he decided to call a vote on the treaty.

But—as he found to his near peril—he almost lost the referendum as $(P_i - I_m)^2$ was considerable; there was little congruence between the president's and elites' preferences for more transfer of sovereignty and the Euroskepticism of large sections of the electorate was considerable.

The same logic, or so it will be argued, can be discerned in the referendums held between 1791 and 1944. To be sure, statistical evidence is hard to come by, but the case studies of historians point in this direction. The first main user of referendums was Napoleon Bonaparte. Though very far from being a believer in democracy, Bonaparte readily submitted policy issues to votes. But more interestingly, when Napoleon was defeated at Waterloo and the Bourbons were reinstalled, they did not seek to justify their return by references to the divine right of kings, nor did they quote Jean Bodin's dictum that "the sovereign Prince is only accountable to God" (quoted in Maritain 1961: 34). Rather, they held a referendum. To be sure, the poll was hardly fair and was, according to a twentieth-century political scientist, "characterized by authoritarian mobilization and fraud" and the "electorate was subjected to strong pressure" (Morel 1996: 68). But the reinstated rulers nevertheless felt a need to have their rule consecrated by a popular plebiscite. Why? What was it that made the plebiscite so suitable to the rulers seeking legitimacy? What was the underlying logic? The referendum can be seen as a mechanism for showing that the government or ruling elite has the support of the people, that their preferences are congruent (Sussman 2006).

Now, showing this is not always politically necessary. It is possible that the views of the governors and the governed are roughly the same. The need to show this congruence emerges only if there is political competition or considerable challengers to the power of the ruling elite. Thus it becomes necessary to show that the views of the rulers and the ruled are close only if the power base of the regime is under threat. For example, to use the example of the French plebiscites at the end of the eighteenth century, the newly established republican regime faced considerable "competition" (i.e., military threats) from both erstwhile royalists in France and the foreign powers that were anything but enthused by the prospect of the new administration in Paris. The challenges to the revolutionaries' rule were considerable. But by holding a referendum on the fate of Avignon in 1791, the Assembly in Paris could show that their actions were close to the views of the people in the areas in question, which gave them legitimacy. Using political science language, the decision to hold a plebiscite provided an opportunity for Paris to show that the preference point of the Assemblée Nationale and that of the median voter in Avignon was small if not congruent. This thinking was evident when the Assembly passed a resolution after the vote in the erstwhile papal enclave, "Considering that the majority of the communes and citizens have expressed freely and solemnly their wish for a union with Avignon and France . . . the National Assembly declares that in conformity with the freely expressed wish of the majority . . . of these two countries to be incorporated into France" (von Martens 1801: 400).

After the defeat of Napoleon and the French (the ideologists of national self-determination), the referendum somewhat lost its appeal, though the rulers who restored monarchy of France did not dare *not* to put the Bourbon rule to a (rigged) vote. They were under pressure and faced competition, and a vote was consistent with the ideal that had gained an axiomatic status after the revolution—that government is founded upon the consent of the governed.

The Risorgimento Referendums

The 1820s and the 1830s were periods of drought in terms of submitting issues to a vote among the people. But the nationalist sentiment regained momentum in the 1830 and did so with a vengeance. In the wake of the reawakened nationalism, a number of irredentist groups began movements that led to a reuse of the idea of the referendum as a mechanism to resolve ethnonational conflict. This was especially true in Italy.

The fragmented Italian states had long wanted unity and unification. Niccolò Machiavelli had dreamed about "seizing Italy and free her from the barbarians" (Machiavelli 2002: 95). While the Italians had been briefly unified under Napoleon, the French emperor had treated Italy as a vassal state (he made his sister, Elisa Baciochi, ruler of Naples, and his son was crowned king of Rome) (Davies 1997: 181).

The Italian nationalists who came of age in the 1830s had a different idea. In his influential treatise *Idea dell'Italia*, Giuseppe Mazzini had plainly said that the "principle of nationality is sacred for me. I regard it as the guiding principle of the future. I am prepared to greet—without fear—any change of the map of Europe, which is the result of a spontaneous manifestation of the will of a people" (quoted in Harder 2006: 29). And as early as 1833, he had proposed that referendums rather than terrorism (as advocated by Filippo Buonarotti) be used to win legitimacy for the project of unification (Mack Smith 1959: 16). Part of the reason for this was, according to Stephen Tierney, a change in ideology: "The demand for increased popular participation grew, [and] the plebiscite became a tool in the independence struggles of the latter part of the century" (Tierney 2012: 62).

These sentiments led to a referendum in Lombardy in May 1848, in which a majority voted to join the Kingdom of Sardinia. This vote was thwarted by the Austrian armies, but a decade later—and with the support of Napoleon III—Austria was forced to concede the territory to the Kingdom of Sardinia. In return for his support, the Italians agreed that two territories, Savoy and Nice (which had been transferred to the Kingdom of Sardinia in 1815), would be allowed to hold plebiscites on whether to join France. Both these votes resulted in large majorities in favor of unification with France. While these referendums were undoubtedly rigged, the same cannot be said of the referendums that—at the insistence of the Italian statesman Conti di Cavour—were held in Tuscany, Emilia, Sicily, Naples, and Umbria. However, the referendums were not the massive manifestations of unquestioned support and high participation rates. As a British envoy in Naples noted, "The proportion of the estimated population actually voting in the plebiscites was a mere 21.17 percent in Tuscany, 20.09 percent in Emilia and 19.17 percent in Naples" (Goodhart 1971: 106).

But why did the Italian Risorgimento rest on referendum? Using the theoretical framework introduced above, the plebiscites proved useful to show that the distance between the people and their rulers—formally ($P_i - I_m)^2$—was small, and at a time when Guiseppe Garibaldi and his allies were threatened by other forces in both Italy and abroad, not least the Austrians and the French (who initially had supported them), there was a need to show that the unification had popular support (Hibbert 1987: 171). While it is not a neat fit, it is difficult to contest the view that the Risorgimento referendums follow some of the logic of the overall model: Garibaldi faced political competition and needed to show that he was close to the people. The referendums were an excellent way of achieving this. In this way, perhaps, the referendum also provided a way of establishing the new state. Massimo d'Azeglio had famously noted that "we have made Italy, it remains to make the Italians" (quoted in Hobsbawm 1992: 3). It is possible that the referendum, as an act of public participation, contributed to the establishment of a new demos.

Nationalist and Separatist Referendums in America

The situation in the United States was less glamorous. The referendum has been deep-seated in American political culture since the War of Independence, and it was used early on in the life of American republic to resolve issues pertaining to sovereignty. The first example occurred in 1788 in Massachusetts. By the mid-1850s it had become commonplace to consult the citizens in major issues of constitutional importance (Lee 1981: 46). Most of these referendums had a deliberative character (Fisch 2006: 485). When the Confederate states turned to plebiscites, the mechanism of direct democracy was used in a hitherto unknown way in North America. So why did some of the southern states resort to referendums?

Like the Italian Risorgimento politicians, the southerners were under severe political pressure and faced considerable competition from the North (Wooster 1961: 117). To maintain legitimacy it was vital for them to show that they understood the concerns of their constituents, and that the voters consented to their actions. A referendum was a convenient way of showing this. Referendums assenting to secession would send a strong signal to Lincoln and the abolitionists in the northern states as well as provide a rallying point for the voters in the South. It is not surprising, therefore, that Texas, Virginia, and Tennessee submitted the decision to secede from the Union to the voters. What is perhaps interesting—and what might show that the decision to hold a referendum was not based on solid facts—is the fact that the support for secession was far from unanimous. In Tennessee,

68 percent voted for secession while 32 percent voted against, and in Texas the figures were 74 percent for and 26 percent against (Mattern 1921: 119).

Schleswig: The Dog That Didn't Bark

After the polls in Italy and the United States, in the middle of the nineteenth century the use of the referendum died down once again. But referendums were proposed. Most notable, perhaps, is the case of the Second Danish-German War of 1864. Following the Danish government's decision to incorporate the two duchies under a Unified Danish Constitution, Prussia and Austria declared war in 1864. After heavy Danish losses, a cease-fire was negotiated in England. During these negotiations "[the] use of a plebiscite had been urged by the British government" (Goodhart 1971: 106). The British proposed that a referendum be held in each of the towns and parishes in the now occupied Schleswig (Ward and Gooch 1923: 579). The German negotiator, Count Albrecht von Bernstorff, declared, "I have nothing against sending this proposal *ad referendum*." However, the chief Danish negotiator, Foreign Secretary Georg Quaade, rejected the proposal and declared that it was against his "instructions" to "submit the matter ad referendum."[1] As a result, hostilities erupted again. The Prussians and the Austrians occupied the whole of Schleswig and—predictably—became less keen on a plebiscite.

But why did the Danes reject the proposal of a referendum? In view of the competition proximity model there is a simple explanation. The Danish public opinion was inflexible, and after the military victory in the Three-Year War against Prussia (1848–51), a large segment of the Danes were in favor of a military solution, which they unrealistically believed would be possible to win. To consent to a referendum would signal that there was a gulf between the position of the government of D. G. Monrad and the people. Formally $(P_i - I_m)^2$ was large. The people did not favor a referendum. There was no strategic mileage in forcing a vote. In addition, Monrad and the National-Liberals had a solid majority and were not challenged electorally. There was little utility in a referendum; consequently, the issue was not sent "ad referendum" (Bak 1975: 274). After the war, Bismarck, in 1866, told the Prussian Parliament that a referendum was necessary. A month later, realizing the significant opposition to German occupation, he annexed the duchies before negotiations over the promised plebiscites could take place. Again, Bismarck's logic was consistent with the competition proximity model; formally $(P_i - I_m)^2$ was large—there was a gulf between Bismarck's position and that of the voters—and Bismarck was under threat neither in the German Reichstag nor internationally. His incentives for holding a referendum were small; nothing would be gained strategically from sending the proposal to the voters, and indeed he might even lose. At this stage, of course, matters had changed considerably in Denmark. Having lost on the battlefield, the Danish government was in were in favor of a referendum. The defeat had not been well received domestically (Monrad had to resign soon after), and a referendum was a popular option—indeed the only option—for regaining the lost territories (Goodhart 1971: 107). This decision not to hold a referendum is in sharp contrast to the Danes' insistence on a referendum on the fate of West Indian islands of Saint Croix, Saint Thomas, and Saint John, which the Americans had offered to buy. Contrary to their opposition to plebiscites in 1864, Copenhagen now argued that a vote was necessary as "a new custom in Europe of holding plebiscites was now so entrenched that any failure to stage a referendum would cause comments" (Goodhart 1971: 109). A referendum was duly held, in which "all male residents, black as white, had a vote. The vote was overwhelmingly in favour of transfer to the United States" (Goodhart 1971: 109).

Nationalist Referendums in the English-Speaking World

The English were never in the vanguard of the movement toward using referendums and plebiscites to resolve national issues. To be sure, the British were not adverse to using the referendum as a tactical means of international politics (e.g., in the case of the referendum in Moldova in 1857, where the referendum was a convenient excuse to curb the influence of the Russian Empire after the Crimean War) and occasionally suggested plebiscites (as they did in the case of Schleswig).

After the Crimean War (which Britain, France, and the Ottoman Empire fought against the Russians), a poll was held to unify the two territories of Moldavia and Walachia (previously an area that had been under Turkish suzerainty, though it was often dominated by Russia under the name Romania) (Laponce 2010: 71). However, it should be noted that the referendum was anything but free and fair; "intimidations and arrests were not infrequent," and up to "nine-tenths of the population were denied the right to vote" (Mattern 1921: 104). Furthermore, the vote was held only after some "bizarres manoevres diplomatiques" (Laponce 2010: 71). While the British were—on occasion—willing to suggest referendums outside their own territories, they were rarely keen to conduct referendums within the empire and its territories.

The British accepted a referendum regarding the transfer of the Ionian Island to Greece (Goodhart 1971: 104), but this was the exception. The government in London—unlike that in Paris—was not smitten by the idea of referendums to resolve issues of sovereignty. Whereas the French willingly submitted the issue of the transfer of sovereignty of Saint Bartholomew from Sweden to France to a plebiscite in 1877 (Mattern 1921: 116), the British were generally opposed to this course of action. In the case of the transfer of sovereignty of Heligoland (an island close to Germany), Lord Salisbury, the foreign secretary, rejected a proposal by Lord Rosebury (later the prime minister) for a plebiscite, stating, "My answer must be negative. The *plebiscite* is not among the traditions of this country. We have not taken a *plebiscite;* and I can see no necessity of doing so" (*House of Lords Debates*, vol. 345, June 1890, columns 1311–12). The same view was taken by Prime Minister William Gladstone, who told Parliament that he was similarly opposed to a referendum. The proposal for a referendum was rejected in the House of Commons by a vote of 172–76 (Mattern 1921: 112).

But this does not mean that the referendum was not used at all by the British, or rather by people of British extraction. Referendums were held in Canada (Nova Scotia), South Africa (Natal), and Australia. The British were keen to give a measure of autonomy to areas with a large white population—such as present-day Canada, Australia, and South Africa. As far as the latter was concerned, a conference was held among the South African colonies with a view to establishing an autonomous union within the British Empire shortly after the Boer War. Based on the recommendations of the conference, the UK Parliament passed the South Africa Act 1909, which was subsequently ratified by the South African colonies. However in Natal, the smallest of the previously existing states, there was considerable concern that a centralized state would be detrimental to the interests of the area. While the South Africa Act was passed in its entirety in the Transvaal and Orange River parliaments, opposition in Natal was so strong that the local administration decided to call a referendum. That settled the issue. Support for union was strong—perhaps because there was little alternative. The South Africa Act was passed 11,121 votes to 3,701 (Kahn 1960: 1).

The establishment of Canada in 1867 did not involve any official referendums. The poll held in Nova Scotia in 1867—on leaving the newly established federation—was an unofficial one and was ignored by the authorities, despite 65 percent voting for separation (Laponce 2010: 50).

The situation was different in Australia, not as a result of British pressure, but because the political class in Australia felt compelled to win support from the constituents before going ahead with the process of federation. That the Australians ratified the unification of their country through a series of plebiscites was not, it seems, due to their British legal and constitutional heritage, but rather a result of the more progressive ideas they had received from another settler society, namely the United States (Williams and Hume 2010: 7).

The 1891 Australian Constitutional Convention agreed that before proceeding with federation, the constitution for governing the new nation should be approved by the people.[2] The intention was affirmed at the Corowa People's Convention in 1893.[3] This enabling legislation was passed in each colony. In 1898 referendums on the Commonwealth Constitution Bill were held in New South Wales, South Australia, Tasmania, and Victoria.

A majority of yes votes was recorded in each colony, but in New South Wales the enabling legislation required a quota of 80,000. This was not achieved. In 1899, as a result of amendments to the constitution recommended by New South Wales, the colonies organized a second round of referendums. This time New South Wales required only a simple majority of yes votes. Queensland also joined the process. Majorities were achieved in all colonies, albeit with different levels of enthusiasm.

There was not widespread support for the federation everywhere. Mineral-rich Western Australia was especially hesitant. By 1900 the colony had still not taken steps to hold a referendum. In protest, residents of the Eastern Goldfields took steps to form a separate colony. This set the ball rolling. Finally, on July 31, 1900, when the Commonwealth Constitution Bill had already been enacted by the British Parliament, a referendum was held in which a large majority voted in favor of federation.

But why were the referendums held in the first place? Was this another case of the logic outlined at the beginning of this chapter? Without wanting to force the matter too far, there are indications that some of the underlying logic was at play. In a famous analysis of the process of federalization

Willian Riker Jr. has pointed out that "external" and "internal" threats are significant (Riker 1975: 116). This was perceived to be the case in Australia. Moreover, there was a need to show that the policy of federation was supported by the voters. Holding a referendum was an ideal way of demonstrating this and was, moreover, consistent with the political fashion at the time, especially as expressed by prominent English lawyers and political theorists (MacIntyre 2004: 138). Yet, as one observer noted, "unlike the Italians, it [Australia] experienced no *Risorgimento*. The turnout in federal referenda was lower than for parliamentary elections" (MacIntyre 2004: 138).

Norway's Vote for Independence, 1905

The most celebrated referendum to be held before World War I was perhaps the 1905 poll in Norway. When Norway's parliament, Stortinget, in 1905 sent notification to Sweden that Norway had seceded from the union established in 1814, the response was initially negative. The Swedish Riksdag responded that the union was two-sided, and that in strict legal terms, the union could not be dissolved without the consent of King Oscar II and the Riksdag (Vedung 2007: 5). Yet the Swedes conceded that the request would be accepted if it was preceded by "a fairly conduced plebiscite" (Nordlund 1905: 365). The statement went on to say that if the "conditions [of a fair referendum] were complied with negotiations would be entered into" (Eden 1905: 23).

The Swedes had not expected that the Norwegian prime minister Christian Michelsen would take up the challenge and organize the referendum. Michelsen, according to a recent study, "had '*teft*'—this strange and almost animalistic ability to sense, feel and gauge things as opposed to the ability to analyse, calculate and rationally assess, even while in the middle of the maelstrom" (Hegge 2010: 97). Michelsen's gamble paid off. More than 99 percent voted to sever the ties between the two countries; Sweden almost immediately entered practical negotiations in the border town of Karlstad and divided the spoils in an amicable way. That this was possible had, perhaps, just as much to do with the fact that the Swedes were not an aspiring power and that the relationship with Norway was not economically or politically beneficial to Stockholm.

But—as area specialists and historians have pointed out—there were also more sinister or strategic reasons behind the referendum. True, Norway was not economically beneficial to the Swedes, but the right-wing parties in the Swedish Riksdag sought to capitalize on the national romanticism among their voters. Seeking to win support in the upcoming Swedish general election in the autumn of 1905, the parties on the right proposed that the issue of the union could be resolved through a referendum. Well aware that the policies of Prime Minister Erik Gustaf Boström had antagonized public opinion in Norway, the parties on the right—especially the Protectionist Party of the Majority—knew "even at the time before mass opinion polls that the Norwegians would vote for independence." However, "calling a referendum could delay matters" and would provide the parties on the Swedish right the opportunity to score party-political points (Bjørklund 2003). The strategy, as suggested by Thomas Wyller, was internal, and the Swedish right was focused on the opportunity to win votes in the upcoming Swedish elections rather than preventing Norwegian independence (Wyller 1992: 40). Seen in this light, it can be argued that the referendum—at least to a degree—conforms to the competition proximity model; the Swedish political parties were competing while locked in to the "competitive struggle for votes," to use Schumpeter's expression (Schumpeter 1942: 242), and the parties on the right knew that public opinion in Sweden favored a delay for nationalistic and romantic reasons. Arguably, the logic of the competition proximity model can be detected. What the parties in Sweden could not have foreseen was Michelsen's "teft" and the Norwegians' ability to organize a referendum in less than two weeks. Furthermore, Michelsen's decision was itself consistent with the model. Under threat from Stockholm, the Norwegian leader faced stiff political competition; and derogatory remarks by Swedish prime minister Erik Gustaf Boström meant that a referendum was a popular option in Norway. Both sides had—at different times—an incentive to call a referendum (Vedung 2007).

Referendums After World War I

It is commonly assumed that Woodrow Wilson was responsible for the referendums in the wake of World War I (Qvortrup 2012). To be sure, before he became president, Wilson (running on a progressive ticket) championed the use of referendums as the people's means of "responding to subsidized machines" (Wilson, quoted in Munro 1912: 87). But while Wilson was still the "enthusiastic apostle of self-determination . . . he had no enthusiasm for plebiscites as such," and, moreover, "this view was shared by the most important members of the American delegation" (Goodhart 1971: 115). That the eight referendums were held to establish the borders between the previously warring states was more a result of internal pressures and strategic considerations (Wambaugh 1933). The British delegation of Lord Balfour (who had advocated the use of referendums to settle the issue of tariff reform in Britain [Bogdanor 1981a: 51]) was at least consistent and was responsible for the referendums that were held. Indeed, it was "the British delegation [that] suggested the plebiscites in Allenstein on the German-Polish border and in Upper Silesia, an area which American experts had originally assigned to Poland" (Goodhart 1971: 115).

It can always be discussed if these referendums resolved the issues of irredentism that so preoccupied the Versailles Conference. Furthermore, the fact that referendums were denied in territories that were claimed by Germany—or in which there was a German majority (e.g., Tyrol and Alsace-Lorraine)—suggests that the referendums were not as neutral and idealistic as some enthusiasts would have us believe. For example, the referendum organized in Tyrol was not endorsed by the Americans, although 90 percent voted for joining Germany. That not all areas were allowed to let the people decide might—with the benefit of hindsight—have paved the way for irredentist claims later. Indeed, it is interesting that—as Vernon Bogdanor has observed—"it was precisely in those areas where plebiscites were refused (with the exception of Alsace-Lorraine)—Danzig, the Polish corridor and the Sudetenland—that were the subject of revisionist claims by the Nazis in the 1930s" (Bogdanor 1981a: 145). And it is equally noteworthy that there were no claims on lands that had decided their allegiance through plebiscites such as Schleswig-Holstein. Even for a dictatorial regime such as Nazi Germany "frontiers that were fixed by plebiscite could not easily be undermined" (Bogdanor 1981a: 145).

The main supporter of referendums after World War I was Germany. The country, which had opposed referendums and plebiscites only a few years before, was now advocating their use whenever given the chance. They did this not only vis-à-vis the Western powers at Versailles but also in their negotiations with the new Soviet regime in the east.

At the negotiations with the Soviet Union at Brest-Litovsk, Austrian foreign minister Graf Czernin proposed to Leon Trotsky, the Soviet foreign minister, that referendums be held in areas currently under the control of German, Austrian, or Turkish troops. The Axis powers affirmed that the future status of Poland and the Baltic States would be decided in "consultation with their populations" (Goodhart 1971: 112). However, only one plebiscite was held under the auspices of the Brest-Litovsk Treaty; in 1918 a referendum was held in Kars (previously a part of the Russian Empire) while it was occupied by Turkish troops. That the Soviet Union had signed up to these conditions did not mean, however, that they were committed to the principle of self-determination. On June 25, 1918, at the Kiev Peace Conference, the Soviet regime signed an agreement with the independent government of Ukraine for a referendum to be held in certain territories claimed by both lands. Two days later, the Red Army—under Trotsky— invaded Ukraine and annexed the whole country without a referendum (Rein 2000: 33).

After World War I, the number of ethnonational referendums dwindled. The votes held between the two world wars outside Germany were largely inconsequential, and in some cases almost political curiosities, such as the referendum in 1933 in Western Australia. On April 8, 1933, the government of premier and Nationalist Sir James Mitchell organized a plebiscite on secession alongside the state parliamentary election. Mitchell campaigned in favor of secession, while the Labor Party campaigned against breaking from the federation. Of the 237,198 voters, 68 percent voted in favor of secession, but at the same time the Nationalists were voted out of office. Only the mining areas, populated by keen Federalists, voted against the move. The state sent a half-hearted petition to the British Parliament requesting independence. It got nowhere after the petition was ruled out of order because the convention dictated that it be made by the Commonwealth (of Australia) and not by the individual state (Williams and Hume 2010: 8). The fact that Mitchell had lost the election effectively killed the proposal. The proposal was stillborn and died away.

The same cannot be said of the votes held in Germany, where Hitler (ab)used the referendum to eliminate differences and to create unity in the Reich. What is perhaps interesting (and disturbing) is that most of these votes—at least according to contemporary observers—were relatively fair. Writing about the referendum regarding withdrawal from the League of Nations, an American observer concluded, "Even after discounting intangible official pressure, of which there undoubtedly was a great deal, and

Table 2. Ethnic and National Referendums, 1918–1945

Country	Area	Year	Difference-eliminating	Difference-managing	Secession	Right-sizing
Russia	Finland	1918			1	
Denmark	Iceland	1918		1		
Turkey	Kars	1918		1		
Austria	Vorarlberg	1919				1
Finland	Aaland	1919				1
Germany	Schleswig I	1920				1
Germany	Schleswig II	1920				1
Germany	Allenstein	1920				1
Belgium	Eupen	1920				1
Germany	Marienwerder	1920				1
Austria	Klagenfurt	1920				1
Germany	Upper Silesia	1921				1
Austria	Tyrol	1921				1
Austria	Salzburg	1921				1
Austria	Sophron	1921				1
United Kingdom	Rhodesia	1922		1		
Australia	Western Australia	1933			1	
Germany	Germany	1933	1			
Germany	Germany	1934	1			
Germany/France	Saar	1935	1			
Germany/France	Germany	1936				1
United States	Philippines	1935			1	
Germany/Austria	Germany/Austria	1938	1			

downright coercion and intimidation at the poll of which there was probably *very little*, the electoral record remains an amazing one" (Zurcher 1935:
95, emphasis added).

In this book we mainly examine referendums after World War II. Up
until this time referendums were to a large degree held for strategic reasons,
often in a way that was consistent with the competition proximity model—
though the evidence analyzed so far is, admittedly, based on impressionistic
evidence drawn from historical accounts by area specialists. Whether the
same conclusion can be drawn if we look more closely at the evidence and
data for the period after 1945 is a matter we seek to answer in the remaining
chapters.

Chapter 2

Difference-Managing Referendums

The difference-managing referendum is a mechanism that limits the scope for action and offers the possibility of what we, paraphrasing the Declaration of Independence, may call the dissent of the governed. Typically, these referendums are held on matters regarding so-called devolution. One of the problems with these referendums is that, to quote Markku Suksi, "there does not exist any solid theory about autonomy or devolution, perhaps because autonomy arrangements are often very pragmatic ad hoc solutions that escape generalisations." Having said this, however, Suksi is happy to accept that devolution normally consists of a situation in which the "inhabitants of the autonomous territory have the right to elect their own self-governing bodies" (Suksi 2003: 21). In this book this definition will be followed.

Generally speaking, difference-managing referendums come in two forms:

> *Devolution referendums*, which deal with the delegation of power (home rule) to a geographically defined territory, like when the Australian Capital Territory was offered self-government in 1978 and like when Nuuk (the capital of Greenland) and Copenhagen submitted their renegotiated relationship to a referendum in 2009.
>
> *Power-sharing referendums*, that is, plebiscites on agreements on consociational power sharing, like the referendum in Burundi in 2005, the plebiscite in Northern Ireland in 1998, and the referendum on power sharing in Suriname in 1987.

But why and when are such referendums held? On one level this is a normative question: difference-managing referendums are held when legitimacy is required for a decision of considerable magnitude and constitutional irreversibility. That, at least, is the theory favored by legal theorists such as A. V. Dicey. Yet, there is also a less idealistic and empirical view, which differs from the normative ideal.

The overall framework of this book proposes that the decision to hold a referendum on an ethnic or national issue, ceteris paribus, follows the competition proximity model.

$$P_{ref} = \sum_{i=1}^{n} \frac{C}{(I_m - P_i)^2}$$

The probability, P_{ref}, that a government, i, will submit a proposal for difference-managing policy (such as, for example, the system of home rule in Scotland) to referendum depends on the relationship between the competition, C, the actor is facing and the squared distance between the government's policy point and the position of the median voter. In the context of difference-managing referendums we would expect that these polls are held when the initiating party, for example the British Labour Party in 1997, was under electoral pressure and if it had reason to believe that its preferred option was close to that of a majority of the voters. For example, in the more empirical literature on British devolution referendums, it is commonly argued that the polls were held for electoral rather than for idealistic or philosophical reasons. In the words of Wyn Jones and Scully, "Mr. Blair's decision was a matter of electoral strategy; neutralizing the potentially contentious part of Labour's constitutional reform agenda as a election issues by allowing the electorate the power of decisions in future referendums" (Wyn Jones and Scully 2012: 15). The Labour Party was locked in competition with the Conservatives. Under the circumstances Labour needed to show that its constitutional reform program coincided with that of the median voter. By promising a referendum on Scottish and Welsh devolution, the government effectively removed the issue—which played well with conservative voters—from the competitive struggle between Labour and the Conservatives.

This model seems convincing—at least superficially—but it is not the only one. We cannot and will not ignore other models that are closer to Dicey's idealistic justification for holding difference-managing referendums. We start with the other contenders.

Dicey: The Referendum as a Constraining Instrument

In a series of articles and papers, including in sixth edition of his influential treatise *An Introduction to the Law of the Constitution* and in the article "Ought the Referendum to be Introduced into England?" (Dicey 1890, 1981), Albert Venn Dicey made a case for the referendum as an "alternative second chamber" (quoted in Qvortrup 1999: 531). Dicey's concern was the policy of home rule for Ireland proposed by William Gladstone's Liberal government.

In 1886, the First Home Rule Bill was proposed, but it was dropped following intense opposition, which split the Liberal Party. After the bill's defeat in the House of Commons, the Second Home Rule Bill was introduced in 1893. This bill was rejected in the House of Lords. But it was gradually becoming clear that the unwritten British Constitution did not have the checks and balances to ensure that radical changes such as this could be prevented.

It was with this in mind that A. V. Dicey—then a professor of constitutional law at All Souls College, Oxford and a staunch conservative—came up with the idea that the referendum could perform the function of an alternative second chamber.

Unlike the House of Lords, the referendum was—in Dicey's opinion— "the one available check on party leaders" and the only institution that could "give formal acknowledgement of the doctrine which lies at the basis of English democracy—that a law depends at bottom for its enactment on the consent of the nation as represented by its electors" (Dicey 1911: 189).

Steeped as he was in the tradition—if not the practice—of liberal constitutionalism, Dicey was at pains to show that the referendum was consistent with the ideal of limited government, but his problem was that the prevailing system, that is, a balance of power between, in his case, the House of Lords and the House of Commons, was out of sync with the realities of popular politics at the time of writing. The political fault line was no longer between the aristocracy and the bourgeoisie, but between the elected representatives and the emerging middle class, which had been granted the vote through different reforms.

In Dicey's view, the elected politicians were not sensitive to this national issue and, through the policy of home rule for Ireland, were in danger of jeopardizing the unity of the nation (as he saw it). The referendum was, in Dicey's view, a mechanism that could put a stop to this, and do so in a way that was consistent with the new doctrine of popular sovereignty. As he wrote,

> I value the referendum first because it is doing away with the strictly speaking absurd system which at present exists, of acting on the presumption that electors can best answer the question raised, e.g. by Home Rule, when it is put together with such totally different questions of prohibition, ... and secondly though in a certain sense mainly because the referendum is an emphatic assertion of the principle that nation stands above parties. (quoted in Cosgrove 1981: 67)

For Dicey, therefore, the referendum was a strictly negative political instrument. It was an instrument that limited the scope of government; it was "nothing more nor less than a national veto" (quoted in Cosgrove 1981: 106).

Of course, Dicey's theory was predominately normative. He was not in the business of predicting when a referendum would be used. He was concerned only with the question of when the people *ought* to be allowed a say on an important issue. And his answer was that the referendum predominately should be held for matters concerning the devolution of power.

At the time of writing—in the late Victorian and early Edwardian age—such referendums were unheard of. As we have seen in Chapter 1, no referendums—with the exception of the referendums in Australia at the turn of the century—were difference-managing referendums. Like Karl Marx, who expected that his theories would be most relevant in developed capitalist societies, Dicey assumed that his normative theory would be most applicable in advanced liberal democracies. However, taking stock of three-quarters of a century of devolution referendums, Rouke, Hiskes, and Zirakzadeh asserted that "referendums on regional self-rule seldom occur in advanced industrialized societies" (Rouke, Hiskes, and Zirakzadeh 1992: 112). Admittedly our focus in this chapter is wider as we consider not only territorial power sharing (e.g., the referendum on the Charlottetown Agreement in Canada in 1992 and the referendum in Catalonia in Spain in 2006) but also nonterritorial consociational agreements such as the Good Friday Agreement in Northern Ireland in 1998.

But nevertheless, the statement does *not* seem to hold true. Looking at the list of difference-managing referendums, most appear to have been held in advanced industrial democracies. Moreover, the assertion that these types of referendums are rare or "seldom occur" is questionable as a 57 difference-eliminating referendums have been held. In fact, 25.9 percent of the 223 ethnonational referendums held since 1791 have fallen in this category.

But Rouke, Hiskes, and Zirakzadeh have a point. Until the late 1970s difference-managing referendums were indeed rare. Apart from the Australian referendums on federation in the late 1890s (and these present a bit of a borderline case, as they concerned the establishment of a new state), very few referendums on managing differences have been held. The referendums on home rule in the U.S. Virgin Islands (1954) and the Polynesian and New Caledonian referendums in 1958 are rare exceptions.

Of the fifty-seven difference-managing referendums, twenty-three were held before 1977, but again almost half of these (eleven) were held in Australia before the turn of the century. If we exclude the Australian federation referendums, it is indeed true that such votes rarely occurred in industrial countries. None of the European or North American capitalist states had referendums that allowed citizens in subordinate territories to vote on schemes of self-government or devolution. The only partial example, the Northern Ireland "Border Poll," can be seen as a partial exception to the rule. However, it is questionable whether the referendum organized by the Conservative British government can be categorized as a difference-managing referendum as it was not preceded by negotiations between Nationalists, on the one hand, and Unionists and the British government on the other.

Indeed, as the question was whether Northern Ireland should become a part of the Irish Republic, it could be argued that the very categorization of the poll is wrong in the first place. But apart from this referendum, no other referendum in this category was held in a developed capitalist society before 1975. Given the futility of the 1973 referendum—it was boycotted by the Nationalist and Republican communities—it is perhaps understandable that the Sunningdale Agreement reached later in the same year was not submitted to a referendum. Interestingly, after 1980 or thereabout, similar agreements have almost always been submitted to the people for ratification. It is this change that seems puzzling. After 1978 a number of countries, most notably Spain, the United Kingdom, Denmark, and Canada, held referendums on self-government for territories seeking a measure of self-government, such as, inter alia, Scotland (1979), Greenland (1979), and the Basque country (1979).

In the period when difference-managing referendums became more common, there seems to have been a shift in the countries that used them. Hitherto these plebiscites were held in overseas territories (Puerto Rico in 1951 is a good example). But since 1979, only a small handful of difference-managing referendums have been held in overseas territories, and most have occurred in the very countries where Rouke, Hiskes, and Zirakzadeh thought they were rare, developed industrial democracies.

But is it generally the case that power-sharing agreements and transfers of powers to devolved parliaments are now submitted to referendums in democratic countries rather than in more authoritarian or less-than-perfect polyarchies?

And if so, can this assertion be sustained and corroborated empirically and statistically? And if the answer is affirmative, can we find an explanation for this pattern? In other words, can we determine when or if difference-managing referendums (DMRs) occur? How can we establish a pattern? Indeed, is there a statistical pattern? Can we determine if Rouke, Hiskes, and Zirakzadeh are wrong? Our hypothesis in this chapter is that DMRs predominately take place in developed democracies rather than in developing autocracies. To render this hypothesis plausible we need to carry out a statistical analysis.

Statistical Analysis of the Occurrence of Difference-Managing Referendums

Before developing this model we need to go back to the fundamental premises. Ethnonational referendums are held in divided societies. Yet, how a society deals with or seeks to resolve the problem of an ethnically divided population is an open question. Leaving aside (for the moment) the problem of irredentist groups (see Chapter 5), we can divide referendums into two categories, according to whether DMRs have been held or not. Using this dichotomous measure as our dependent variable we can—using logistic regression analysis—correlate the presence of DMRs with a number of different independent variables, namely the level of democratization (measured by Freedom House scores), economic development (measured by GDP per capita in the year of the referendum), ethnic fractionalization, and the type of democracy (consensus or majoritarian democracy). The latter will be measured by a proxy—the Laakso-Taagepera effective number of

*Box 2. New Caledonia: The Referendum as a Mechanism
for Defusing Tensions?*

In the 1970s, the Kanak independence movement was launched. It drew steady support from other countries in the region and grew stronger in the 1980s. In 1984 the Front de Libération Nationale Kanak et Socialiste (FLNKS) was founded as an umbrella organization for the proindependence parties, and later that year FLNKS established a provisional independent government. However, tensions continued to grow, and between 1984 and 1988 around eighty people died in clashes and terrorist attacks (Aldrich 1993). In response to this the French government initiated negotiations with a view to a settlement. These negotiations were concluded with the Matignon Accords in 1988 among FLNKS, the loyalist Rassemblement pour une Calédonie dans la République (RPCR), and the French government. The Matignon Accords provided for greater local autonomy (including provincial governments) and substantial aid designed to redress deep inequalities between the French and Kanak communities, while committing the territory to a self-determination referendum ten years later. The Matignon Accords— negotiated by the French prime minister M. Michel Rocard—were approved in a referendum in 1988. They were supported by 88 percent of the voters.[1] In 1998 the three Matignon Accords partners agreed on a new statute defining the territory's institutions and its relations with France. The agreement, termed the "Nouméa Accord," steered a middle course between the respective political aspirations of the RPCR and FLNKS, and avoided the need for a divisive yes-no referendum on independence. It was signed on May 5, 1998, during a visit to New Caledonia by the French prime minister Jospin, and approved by 72 percent of New Caledonians in a referendum on November 8, 1998. The accord was subsequently ratified by the French National Assembly and Senate. As a result, New Caledonia is no longer a French Overseas Territory but has its own special status as a *collectivité* within the French Constitution (Bensa 2003).

However, the same trick did not work for President Jacques Chirac, who sought to use a referendum on a modest proposal for more autonomy— negotiated by Nicolas Sarkozy—for Corsica in 2003. The turnout was low (54 percent), and the proposal received only 48 percent support.[2] Perhaps needless to say, violence has continued.

Table 3. Regression Models of Difference-Managing Referendums

Variable	Model I	Model II	Model III[a]
Ethnic fractionalization	−0.614	−0.630*	0.13
	(0.402)	(4.19)	(0.190)
Effective number of parties	0.298		−0.029
	(0.56)		(0.056)
Freedom House score	0.17***	2.08***	0.185***
	(0.030)	(0.821)	(0.030)
GDP per capita	0	0	0
	(0)	(0)	(0)
Civil rights	−0.417**		
	(2.3)		
Constant	24.9**	14.5**	1.38***
	(12.7)	(6.20)	(0.32)
N	59	59	59
r^2	.92	.92	.81

Note: Values are coefficients (standard errors in parentheses). Wald scores for Model I: 3.2 (civil rights) and 2.2 (ethnic fractionalization). Wald score for Model II: 6.42 (Freedom House score).
[a] Linear (ordinary least squares regression).
*Significant at .10.   **Significant at .05.   ***Significant at .01.

parties (ENP). Of course it would have been better to use Lijphart's measure, but this is not available for most countries (Lijphart 2012). However, as there is a near perfect match between Lijphart's consensus index and the ENP, it is justified to use the latter. Formally speaking the probability that a difference-managing referendum will be held in country i can formally be expressed as

$$P_{DMR} = \sum_{i=1}^{n} FH + GDP + \text{Ethnic Fractionalization} + ENP$$

The question is if the Freedom House score—and possibly the ENP—is statistically stronger than the other variables. Provided this is the case, we can begin to further analyze the background and add empirical meat to the bare bones presented in the statistical analyses. The results of the statistical analyses are presented in Table 3.

Based on the regression models, the logistic as well as the linear ones (though using the latter is, arguably, methodologically unsound as the dependent variable is dichotomous), the conclusion seems to be that DMRs are significantly more likely to occur in countries with a high level of political freedom, that is, in countries that have a score of less than two on the seven-point Freedom House Index.

The Freedom House variable is statistically significant at the .001 level in Model III and at the .05 level in Model II. Given the small standard error in both models, there is strong evidence that the decision to hold difference-managing referendums is correlated with the level of political freedom. Hence the argument proposed by Rouke, Hiskes, and Zirakzadeh seems to be falsified when subjected to statistical analysis.

Perhaps we would have expected there to be more examples of difference-managing referendums in very divided societies. After all, this type of the referendum is held to manage ethnic strife and differences. Interestingly, there is not a strong correlation between the ethnic fractionalization index and the presence of DMRs, and the ethnic fractionalization variable is just above the 10 percent level of statistical significance in all but one of the models. While all the countries that have held referendums on ethnonational issues have high levels of ethnic fractionalization, that is, are ethnically diverse, there is only a small indication that a higher level of fractionalization increases the probability of holding DMRs.

Rouke, Hiskes, and Zirakzadeh's other assertion, namely that difference-managing referendums are uncommon in developed industrial societies, is similarly falsified. With development measured by GDP per capita—a good proxy for whether a country is developed or not—we find that this factor is statistically insignificant in all the models. A high GDP per capita neither increases nor decreases the probability of DMRs.

So, the level of political freedom is the strongest factor explaining—at least statistically—the presence of difference-managing referendums. But we can find more than that! Using logistic regression, we can measure the likelihood (i.e., probability) of something happening. Based on the calculations we find that for every one-unit improvement in the Freedom House score there is a six times greater probability that a referendum will be held in an ethnically diverse society. That this calculation is statistically significant at the 1 percent level means that this relationship is present in 99 percent of the cases; in other words the initial hypothesis that higher levels of democracy are correlated with difference-managing referendums is corroborated statistically.

Given the strength of the correlation between Freedom House scores and DMRs we can concentrate on the finding that higher levels of political freedom lead to higher chances of difference-managing referendums being held. As we have seen, some of the most prominent DMRs have been held in democratic countries. In Canada the Charlottetown Agreement was submitted to a vote in 1992. And in Spain between 1979 and 1981—and later in 2006 (Catalonia) and 2007 (Andalucía)—schemes of difference-managing policies were submitted to voters, as were, as we have seen, various policies regulating the relationship between the center and the periphery in the United Kingdom. But in less democratic countries similar schemes of difference-managing policies were not submitted to referendums. The devolution granted to Tobago in 1980 was not submitted to a referendum, nor have the inhabitants of Aceh in Indonesia been granted a right to vote on a scheme of home rule (Ross 2005: 35). Given that democratic countries tend to hold devolution referendums, one might ask why the scheme for self-government for Südtyrol (Alto Adige) in Italy was not submitted to a referendum when this was established by the Austro-Italian Treaty in 1971? The answer is perhaps that the doctrine that such matters have to be ratified by referendum had not yet taken root. It is certainly interesting that the proposed federalization of Italy in 2006, which 61 percent of voters rejected, was submitted to a referendum (Pinelli 2006). But it is also possible that no referendum was held because there was no strategic reason for holding one. There was no electoral threat to the governing parties at the time, save from the—in Sartori's sense—"irrelevant parties" (Evans 2002: 157). Hence, the incentives for holding a referendum were—consistent with the competition proximity model—limited.

We have already looked at the example of the United Kingdom, where it has become a convention of the constitution that policies of difference management are submitted to referendums. But is there a reason why this norm seems to have been established in countries that have a high level of democratic and civil freedoms such as Spain and Canada?

There is some anecdotal evidence that the decision to hold referendums on devolution in Spain in the post-Franco era was a deliberate attempt to break with the authoritarian past (Gunther, Sani, and Shabad 1988: 249). Similarly, in Canada the decision to hold a referendum on the Charlottetown Agreement was a deliberate attempt to show that the perceived elitism of the failed Meech Lake Agreement—which failed after a filibuster in the Manitoba Assembly—could be remedied only by the people's direct involvement in a referendum. In the words of Ronald Watts, "The Constitution does not require a referendum for ratification of constitutional amendments, but during 1992 the conviction developed among the negotiating governments that popular support indicated by a favorable consultative referendum result would facilitate ratification by the required legislatures by giving the proposals political legitimacy" (Watts 1999: 5).

But these anecdotal facts and the statistical support for the model do not conclusively prove that DMRs tend to be held in countries with the highest levels of democratic freedom. As pointed out in the more philosophical literature ever since Al-Ghazali's *Incoherence of Philosophy* and the work of William of Ockham (Scruton 1995: 126)—and indeed before[3]—a numerical correlation does suggest that there is a causal relationship; the statistical fact that there is a statistical association does not prove the thesis. All too often political scientists enamored by—or in awe of—statistical models are content with settling for a statistical relationship without inquiring about the plausibility of underlying causes.

What is necessary from a social science point of view is not merely to establish a numerical relationship but also to come up with an explanation. Following our Popperian—or hypothetical-deductivist—model, it is moreover imperative that we explain outliers without resorting to ad hoc hypotheses.

What we have established through our statistical model is that ethnically diverse societies with high levels of political freedom are significantly more likely to submit difference-managing policies to referendums. This relationship amounts to a general hypothesis of the *modus tollens* form (see the Introduction). But the question is if this model—this hypothetical syllogism—can be supported by facts or if it should be considered falsified by the presence of deviant cases. Furthermore, the question is if this tendency is consistent with—or contradicts—the competition proximity model. Before considering this it is noteworthy that for the most part, difference-managing referendums fall in the expected categories. The referendums in Wales in 1979, 1997, and 2011 took place in countries that were established, consolidated, and universally recognized polyarchies. The same is true for the referendums in Canada (Nunavut 1998), Denmark (Greenland 2009), and France (New Caledonia 1988). But what about the referendums that do not fall into the expected categories. What about Suriname 1987, the Philippines 1989, and Burundi 2005? To stay true to our falsificationist approach we need auxiliary hypotheses that are universal rather than ad hoc. If we do not we are—in following Popper's approach—forced to reject the whole hypothesis and start over.

There are several examples that stand out and call for an explanation, though some more than others. The fact that Burundi held a referendum on a power-sharing agreement in 2005 would appear to be an anomaly. Yet with a relatively democratic system (Freedom House score = 3), the African country is not a clear anomaly. Having emerged from a period of authoritarian rule (the country had a Freedom House score of 7 in the 1990s), Burundi is not much different from Spain in 1979, when the latter country held a series of DMRs and was rated with a Freedom House score of 2. The fact of the matter, as far as Burundi is concerned, is that its democratic system was in the process of becoming more democratic as a result of the agreement that had been reached between the Tutsies and Hutu groups under the transitional government of Domitien Ndayizeye (Basedeau 2011: 205).

The same argument holds true for the referendums in Suriname in 1987 and in the Philippines in 1989 and 1990. In the latter case, the fall of the Marcos regime opened up a demand for a resolution of the territorial and regional disputes that had been kept under wraps during the years of authoritarian rule and under the policies of difference elimination that had been initiated with the referendum in 1977 (Machado: 1978: 202). The problem with the 1989 referendum in the Philippines was that Filipinos were split along religious lines: "while the four Muslim-dominated provinces were in favour all the nine Christian dominated provinces were against" (He 2002: 75). This split arguably exacerbated the differences between the two communities.

The fact that the Philippines was "partly free" (Freedom House score = 3) in 1989 and that the country's status had improved to "mostly free" a year after (when the second referendum was held) suggests that the country was in a process of democratization. All of this supports the case and the auxiliary hypotheses that difference-eliminating referendums may occur in countries that are not among the highest in Freedom House scores if the country is in the process of democratization.

The same is arguably true for Suriname (MacDonald 1988: 105). Suriname—like the Philippines, Burundi, and, indeed, Spain in 1979—was a country in transition, although its Freedom House score was rather low (Freedom House score 1987 = 4). But this figure soon improved. Already the following year the country had improved by one point to "partly free." To be sure the process of democratization in Suriname was uneven and marred by setbacks, yet the country was in the process of the democratization that culminated in 1999, when the country was categorized as "free." We thus have to modify the original hypothesis to this: "difference-managing referendums occur in countries with regionally based ethnic differences that are democratic or democratizing." This model, as it will be seen, is consistent with the methodological criterion that the auxiliary hypothesis (in this case the process of democratization) is universal and independently testable.

But how does the conclusion that DMRs tend to occur in polities that have favorable Freedom House scores square with the competition proximity model? Are they compatible? One possibility could be that DMRs occur in more democratic states precisely because there is more competition in these polities and because the initiators of referendums need to show that their policies on managing ethnic and national tension are consistent with the median voter in a democratic country where the fate of the rulers can be terminated at the ballot box.

For example, case studies have shown that the Welsh referendum in 2011 (on whether to give the Welsh Assembly the power to pass primary legislation) was initiated because First Minister Rhodri Morgan faced completion from elected Labour politicians, "many of whom remained deeply skeptical about devolution" (Wyn Jones and Scully 2012: 15). This competition—and the fact that close to 75 percent of the voters wanted a Welsh Assembly with primary legislative powers (Wyn Jones and Scully 2012: 70)—meant the Morgan's preference point was closer to that of the median voters than was the position of the elected MPs, who feared that they might lose their seats at Westminster if the Assembly's powers were strengthened. But what does the statistical evidence say? Overall, there is evidence for the thesis that the competition proximity model provides an explanation for the occurrence of DMRs.

When taking the dummy variable competition (1 if the initiator is under electoral threat as defined by opinion polls or 0 if not) and the support for the measures (as provided by national opinion polls), we are able to empirically test the competition proximity model's explanatory value as regards DMRs.

Arguably, this research design is a bit impressionistic, but nevertheless using logistic regression—justified as the dependent variable is dichotomous—we find that the measures for the competition proximity model both are statistically significant and have higher explanatory value than the Freedom House variable. This result is also found when using ordinary least squares regression (though this method is less appropriate as the dependent

Table 4. Competition Proximity Model for Difference-Managing Referendums

Variable	Model I
Freedom House score	0.408*
	(0.67)
Competition	5.092**
	(2.3)
Support	0.39*
	(0.02)
Constant	−0.455*
	(3.53)
N	43
Pseudo-r^2	.76

Standard errors in parentheses.
Source: Data based on Gallup and IPSOS Mori national polls (http://www.ipsos-mori.com/
Search.aspx?usterms = Elections, accessed December 12, 2012).
*Significant at .1.   **Significant at .05.

variable is binary). The statistical evidence thus supports the overall conclusion that difference-eliminating referendums occur in democratic countries
and, more importantly, tends to do so especially when the initiator is facing
political competition. Indeed, in Model I, there is a fivefold increase in the
probability of a difference-managing referendum taking place if the initiator is facing electoral competition. Whereas Freedom House scores add to
the model, competition scores the highest in the logistic regression model.
Based on the statistical calculations, the variables of the competition proximity model support the case studies we analyzed in the previous chapter.

Conclusion

Since the 1980s difference-managing referendums have tended to occur in
industrial countries with high Freedom House scores. But why is this case?
Some would argue that referendums of this kind have been held not out of
self-interest (or the logic of consequentiality) but as a result of an understanding prevalent in democratic societies that issues that concern the sharing of power are so fundamental that they must be submitted to the people
for their approval. But simple bivariate correlations do not tell the full
story. A more sophisticated model suggests that yes, difference-managing
referendums tend to occur in democratic polities, but they are much more
likely to occur when the government or the initiator is under electoral theat.

Box 3. The Establishment of the Swiss Canton of Jura in the 1970s

Difference-managing referendums can be carried on almost *ad absurdum*. This was perhaps the case in Switzerland in the 1970s. Between 1974 and 1978 a series of referendums took place to determine if the French-speaking minority in the Canton of Berne should be allowed to form their own new canton (Laponce 2001). The problem had started many years before at the Congress of Vienna—where precious little thought was given to national and ethnic groups and where the powers were keen on restoring the pre-Napoleonic order (Kissinger 1957). The conservative, mainly Catholic, and French-speaking Jura—once an "autonomous political entity"—was joined with the liberal, German-speaking, and Protestant Canton of Berne (Buechi 2012: 187). After several unsuccessful attempts to establish a new canton—including a failed citizen initiative in 1959—the cantonal government in Berne decided to put the matter to a referendum (Buechi 2012: 189). Initially the entire population of the canton was asked in 1973 to endorse—or otherwise—that a referendum could be held in the enclave of Jura (the area of the proposed new canton). The Berne administration was under pressure, but the "expectation was that, as in 1959, a majority would vote against the creation of the new canton of Jura" (Buechi 2012: 189). The result of this poll was a narrow majority in support of the establishment of a new canton—51 percent voted yes, with 88 percent turnout! (turnout in Swiss referendums is normally below 50 percent) (Lutz and Marsh 2007). However, the referendum showed a split between the French-speaking Protestants in the southern part of Jura, who wanted to remain part of Bern. But support was strong among the French-speaking Catholics, who were in favor of establishing a new canton, and thus in favor of splitting from their German-speaking co-religionists. To resolve the impasse, "citizen initiated referendums in favour of remaining in the canton of Berne were now organised [in the three southern districts]" (Buechi 2012: 191). This second referendum rejected the proposition, and the net result was that the three northern districts of Jura formed a new canton, whereas the three southern districts remained part of Berne. After the vote, a further thirteen citizen-initiated local votes were held along the new cantonal border; "[5] majority Protestant districts voted to remain with Berne and 8 majority Catholic districts opted for the Jura" (Buechi 2012: 191). As if this were not enough, the establishment of the new canton of Jura was ratified in a federal referendum, and those in the new canton voted for a new cantonal constitution in a referendum.

So why did the authorities hold a referendum? There is some suggestion that the initial vote in 1973 was held for strategic reasons that were not inconsistent with the competition proximity model (Mayer 1968). However, it is not a neat fit, and in any case the citizen-initiated referendums that followed were held for other reasons, namely in order to get recognition for different minorities' rights. The model does not account for citizen-initiated votes, nor does it account for constitutionally mandatory referendums. But this limitation in the theoretical model notwithstanding, the referendum worked; the Jura issue that was created by elitist bargaining in 1815 was resolved by citizen-initiated referendums in the 1970s.

Other scholars using less positivist methods have found that "democratization has facilitated conditions under which referenda can be adopted and accepted as a means of settling [questions]. The ideas of popular sovereignty and the referendum principle emerge when countries embark upon democratization" (He 2002: 71). This conclusion is correct, but it needs to be added that democratization was not the only factor. It is possible that a more democratic society was a necessary condition, but the trigger that led to referendums was political competition and the perceived popular support for the measures being proposed. The move toward democracy did not lead to a more idealistic politics or amicable agreement but forced political elites to take into account the views of the voters. In short, more democracy leads to more competition, which, in turn, leads to more democratic involvement.

Chapter 3

Secession and Partition

As long as our world is made up of national groups which aspire to
self-governance and to territorial sovereignty, ours will be a world of
sovereign states and secessions from them.
—Pavkovic and Radan (2007: 256)

"Secession," according to Aleksandar Pavkovic and Peter Radan, is a "process of withdrawal of a territory and its population from an existing state and the creation of a new state on that territory" (Pavkovic and Radan 2007: 1). Needless to say, secession is a process of far-reaching and irreversible consequences. Once undertaken, the process of a political divorce between two groups sharing the same territory is a one-way street—one that often has a violent aftermath. No countries that have split up, or from which one part has seceded, have become unified. There are not political equivalents of Richard Burton and Elizabeth Taylor (who famously remarried), though Yemen came close (and pace Germany).[1] Because of the far-reaching and irreversible character of secessions, it is—in an era of popular sovereignty—natural that such changes are expected to be ratified by the voters. John Stuart Mill—writing in *Considerations on Representative Government*—was an early and perhaps unwitting exponent of this view, when he stressed that "where the sentiment of nationality exists in any force, there is a prima facie case for uniting all the members of the nationality under the same government. . . . This is merely saying that the question of government ought to be decided by the governed" (Mill 1980: 234).

In other words, the people—the citizens of a particular territory—should have the final say due to the magnitude and irreversibility of the decision. But does the decision to hold referendums on independence follow this ideal, or are referendums more likely to be the result of tactical considerations as suggested by the competition proximity model?

Like in the other chapters discussed in this book, a case can be made for the view that referendums on independence followed a rational, self-interested, logic rather than an idealistic one. Applying once again the competition proximity model, it is—as it will be argued in this chapter—possible, for example to see the decision to hold a referendum on independence for Bosnia-Herzegovina as an example of this model in practice. The Bosnian leadership faced competition—and a military threat—from stronger actors within the Yugoslav Federation, in particular Serbia. However the Bosnians also knew that there was support for independence among a majority of those living in the state (Bringa 1993). In other words, and once again using the formal language, $(I_m - P_i)^2$ was perceived to be small and C was perceived to be large, and it was rational to hold a referendum. Whether the model works as neatly in other places and whether it is supported by statistical evidence across cases are matters that will be considered here.

For a while, especially in the 1970s and the 1980s, it seemed that this kind of referendum had become a thing of the past. In the words of an international lawyer, "The notion that the right of self-determination embraces a legitimate claim to independent statehood seemed to have fallen into desuetude with a decolonisation process."[2] This can no longer be said. After the deluge of referendums at the beginning of the 1990s and more recently the referendums in Montenegro (2006) and Southern Sudan (2011), self-determination referendums are back in business. Whether that is a good or a bad thing is a matter of taste, and it should be said at the outset that no two secession referendums are the same. Sometimes these plebiscites lead to hostilities, and other times they are resolved amicably. This is an issue we examine in this chapter. But before we do so we need to determine when such referendums are held at all.

The Comparative Study of Secessions

There have been many different referendums on secession. This is one of the problems for the social scientist who deals with generalizations. For it is, on the face of it, difficult to compare the Latvian referendum in 1991, the referendum in French Guinea in 1958, and the plebiscite in Iceland in

1945. Add to these examples the case of Southern Sudan in 2011 and the picture seems blurred, messy, and downright confusing.

There is no point in seeking a pattern where there is none. The aim of the social sciences is not the identification of spurious commonalities. There are issues that defy classification. Yet sometimes what seems to be a mishmash of factors actually does form a pattern. G. W. F. Hegel, not normally someone associated with positivist sentiments, spoke in awe of social science, which "dissects the laws of apparently random occurrences." And he found it "noteworthy to see connections, which one at first glance would have thought did not exist, are in fact the consequence of individual factors [*Wilkür*]. The [social sciences] are thus like the planetary system, which appears—at first glance—to be unregulated and random, but which are, in fact, subject to laws" (Hegel 1832/1976: 347). Needless to say, we may not be able to repeat the feat of the social sciences of Hegel's time (he was writing about political economy!), but the ambition should be there, and—being optimists—we have (the differences above notwithstanding) reason to believe that there may be more of a common pattern than may at first glance appear to be the case.

Here we consider "political divorce settlements." These are concerned with secession and partitions. Since the American Civil War—when, inter alia, Texas and Tennessee voted to leave the union—scores of referendums have been held on whether territories should secede. Sometimes these divorces are amicable—at other times they are acrimonious and bitter. Sometimes they result in peaceful resolutions of long-standing conflicts (e.g., in the case of Norway in 1905). But more often than not, these polls result in exacerbated conflicts and deepening tensions (as was the case in Bosnia-Herzegovina and East Timor).

Divorce Settlements and Referendums

Generally speaking it has become an accepted norm in international relations that erstwhile colonies should be granted independence after referendums. This was not always the case, and this change represents a break with earlier epochs, when "the rules governing the intercourse of states [did] neither demand nor recognize the application of the plebiscite in the determination of sovereignty" (Mattern 1921: 171). This has changed. Referendums are now (once again) seen as de rigueur and a political *conditio sine*

> **Box 4. *The Secessionist Referendum in Southern Sudan 2011***
>
> After a war lasting for decades, a referendum was held on independence in Southern Sudan between January 9 and January 15, 2011. The vote—which was stipulated as a part of the 2005 comprehensive peace agreement—was not without drama. The National Congress Party (which represents the largely Muslim north) suggested in negotiations that at least 75 percent had to vote in favor for the referendum to be valid. The SPLM/A (representing the predominately Christian and animist south) argued that no special requirement was necessary. In October 2009, the central government of Sudan and the South Sudanese government agreed that turnout would have to be at least 60 percent of the 3.8 million voters to validate the result. In this case, a simple majority vote in favor of independence would trigger a second referendum within sixty days should the turnout be insufficient in the first referendum. Sudan's President Omar al-Bashir said that the southern region had a right to choose to secede and that the referendum was helpful because unity "could not be forced by power." In the referendum the vast majority of the voters in Southern Sudan (98.83 percent) voted in favor of independence. The turnout exceeded 60 percent by a considerable margin.

qua non in cases where a defined part of an existing state wishes to become independent (Beigbeder 1994: 91). UN secretary general Ban Ki-moon and his predecessors have on several occasions urged that former (and still existing) colonial powers complete the decolonization process in every one of the remaining sixteen non-self-governing territories. The recognition that all former colonies and dependent territories should be "free" was the formal justification for the referendums on independence in, respectively, Eritrea (1993) and East Timor (1999)—though not in the referendum in Southern Sudan (2011). The former areas had been self-governing and were perceived to be (or were argued to be) "colonies." Hence, they were allowed to become independent states.[3] As noted this, was not the case in Southern Sudan (Box 4).

Secession Referendums and the Breakdown of the International Order

But what we are looking for here is a general pattern, a "social science law" to use Hegel's expression. Our first hypothesis is that secession referendums are held after momentous changes in the international system, when great powers weaken. And the other theory, of course, is the competition proximity model. We shall analyze each in turn.

We base this first hypothesis on impressions and tendencies. In several countries, such as, for example, Latvia and the Faroe Islands (Box 5), referendums were held after momentous political changes.

The vote in the Faroe Islands is one of only two examples of successful referendums that have not led to independence (the other being Western Australia, a decade and a bit earlier). But before looking at a more formal model, it might be instructive to look at examples of countries that did not hold referendums.

In Ireland there was talk about a referendum immediately after independence was won; "the independence movement *Sinn Féin*'s policy was to secure Ireland's independence first and allow the people to then choose its own form of government in a referendum" (Kissane 2012: 145), but— perhaps for strategic reasons, or perhaps due to the civil war that broke out soon after—no referendum was held before 1937. This pattern was a repeat of what had happened in Finland a few years earlier.

Finland had been a relatively autonomous part of Russia until World War I. But the fall of the tsarist regime meant that Finland had an opportunity to shake off the Russian shackles. The new Russian leaders, the Bolsheviks, were busy maintaining control of the territory. Lenin and Stalin thought that at the end of 1917 there should be a referendum in Finland on the independence issue and that such a vote would result in a situation in which Finland would decide to join the new socialist state in the east. But nothing came out of it (Kirby 1974: 63). Why? What explains the Finns' decision *not* to hold a referendum? For a start, the collective noun "Finns" is misplaced. The demos was far from a unified or even monolithic block. The leader of the independence movement, P. E. Svinhufvud, faced considerable competition domestically, especially from the Social Democrats, and externally from the newly established Soviet Union (Räikkönen 1938: 12). However, there was nothing that suggested that a popular vote was a strongly demanded policy among the Finns. Indeed, Svinhufvud faced considerable opposition among large segments of society, something that led to the civil war, which cost the lives of 37,000 people (Alapuro 1988: 88). Holding a referendum would not necessarily have increased the legitimacy of Svinhufvud and the *valkoiset* ("the whites") vis-à-vis the Social Democrats and the "reds" (*punaiset*). Hence a referendum was *not* held.

Box 5. *The Faroe Islands: The Independence That Never Was*

When Denmark got its first democratic constitution, the Juni-Grundloven, in 1849, Iceland decided to reject an offer to ratify the new constitution and get six members of the Danish Folketing (Parliament) in return. Instead Iceland opted for a confederal relationship (Lindal 2003: 184).

The other North Atlantic territory under the Danish Crown, the Faroe Islands, apparently without much deliberation, and no consultation at all, was granted the status of a Danish county despite its distinct language, history, and culture (Sølvará 2003: 156). (Another Danish territory, Greenland, had the status of a colony and was governed directly by Copenhagen.)

The fact that the Faroese people were not consulted was strongly criticized by the leader of the Faroese independence movements, Jóhannes Patursson, when the nationalist movement gained ground at the beginning of the twentieth century. However, it is questionable if the voters on the islands would have rejected the offer to be part of Denmark if they had been given the chance. The Faroese were politically inactive, and most were oblivious to the changes (Sølvará 2003: 159).

Despite Patursson's efforts, unionism was the strongest political force on the islands, and the Unionist Party was the largest party. A majority of the voters were keen not to jeopardize the relationship with the parent country. This unionist sentiment manifested itself in curious ways. In 1916, when the Danish (and Faroese) voters were asked to ratify the sale of the Danish West Indies to the United States, a majority of 64 percent of all voters said yes. Only one county voted no, with the Faroe Islands returning a no vote of 67 percent. The Faroese voters were aware that they were a drain on the Danish treasury and were afraid that the Danes would sell them to the highest bidder (Sølvará 2010). In the 1930s, nationalist sentiment and demand for independence grew. As a result, and partly to call the separatists' bluff, the Danish prime minister, Thorvald Stauning, offered that the Faroese could hold a referendum on independence, but the proposal came to nothing. Demand for independence continued to grow, although the Unionist Party maintained a majority in the Faroese Assembly. In 1939, the center-right separatist party Fólkaflokkurin was established. When Denmark was occupied by the Germans in April 1940, the Fólkaflokkurin immediately called for independence. This was rejected by the other parties that had a majority of the seats in the assembly (Løgtingið). During World War II the Faroe Islands were under British protection, but internally the islands were governed by the prefect (Amtmand) and the Løgtingið. During this time the islands were governed by a provisional law (*midlertidig styrelsesordning*, temporary governance mechanism). This empowered the assembly to pass legislation. The Amtmand came up with the name and decided not to use the word

Box 5. *(continued)*

Styrelseslov, as the word *lov* (law or act) indicated that the Faroese Assembly had usurped legislative powers from the Danes. During the war the islands thrived economically by selling fish to the British, and partly as a result, support for independence grew. This support led to the Fólkaflokkurin winning a the 1943 election, though they were one seat short of an absolute majority. At end of World War II both Copenhagen and Tórshavn agreed that the status quo ante was not viable. The Danes offered the Faroese a limited measure of home rule—known as "the Danish proposal"—to replace the prewar status. This was seen as insufficient by the Faroese government. Fólkaflokkurin, as the largest party in the Løgtingið, decided to hold a referendum on the issue. But why?

There are few definite historical accounts, and the archives do not reveal the full story, but from what historians have pieced together, it is clear that Fólkaflokkurin, as the only secessionist party, was faced with immense completion from the unionist parties and, indeed, from Copenhagen where the new center-right government of Knud Kristensen had campaigned on a nationalist platform that envisaged even revisionist claims against Germany (Hammerich 1976: 60). At the same time there were strong indications that the vast number of voters in the islands wanted, if not outright independence, at least a much looser relationship with Copenhagen (Sølvará 2003: 156). As such, the decision to hold a referendum followed the familiar pattern, and it seems—if we could measure it—that

$$P_{ref} = \sum_{i=1}^{n} \frac{C}{(I_m - P_i)^2} > 1$$

That is, the independence party was under threat but had a popular policy. It is not surprising that Fólkaflokkurin opted for a referendum.

In most referendums the voters have a choice between a new policy or no change. The Faroese *fólkaatvøður* (plebiscite) was different. Officially there were no yes or no votes on the referendum in 1946. The voters were asked to put a cross (X) for either the Danish proposal or separation. But the leader of Fólkaflokkurin, Thorstein Petersen (the official leader was Jóhannes Patursson, but he was eighty years old in 1946 and died on August 2 the same year), officially told voters who were not convinced about secession, but strongly against the Danish proposal, to vote against this. According to Petersen this signaled a third choice. Perhaps as a result of this the number of invalid votes was high at 4.1 percent. To the surprise of everyone, not least the separatists, the latter option won a narrow majority; 50.7 percent supported independence. The Danish prime minister, Knud Kristensen, said he accepted the result and the Fólkaflokkurin, which had a majority along

Box 5. (continued)

with a single defector from the Social Democrat Party, began to implement the result. However, Kristensen fell ill. And the Amtmand (Prefect) Carl Aage. Hilbert threw a constitutional spanner in the works of the secessionists. Invoking Article 20 of the Løgtingiðloven 1924 (Assembly of the Faroe Islands Act 1924), he pointed out that the referendum was merely advisory. In order to resolve the matter, Danish King Christian X dissolved the Løgtingið. In the subsequent election, the Unionist Party won a comfortable majority.

This majority negotiated a far-reaching agreement between Copenhagen and Tórshavn, according to which the Faroe Islands were granted home rule in most areas apart from defense and foreign affairs but kept their two members in Danish Parliament. The result of the vote in 1946 was not independence, although a small majority had voted for this. But it is arguably the case that the devolution that resulted from the negotiations was closer to the preference of a majority of the voters. The referendum in 1946 thus paved the way for a compromise that most voters, at the time at least, wanted (Thorsteinson and Rasmussen 1999: 513).

A different pattern can be observed roughly seventy years later, when Finland's southern neighbor Latvia broke free from the Soviet Union. On March 3, 1991, 73 percent of those who voted (87 percent turnout) endorsed the proposition, "Are you in for a democratic and independent Republic of Latvia?" Why? Perhaps because the conditions of the competition proximity model were met. The separatists knew that their position was congruent with that of large segments of society. Faced with a continuing threat of military force from Moscow, the leadership opted for a referendum, conscious that a majority vote would give them legitimacy. The conditions for holding a referendum were certainly met (Karklins 1994: 61). These examples show that secessionist referendums can follow the logic of the competition proximity model, but the latter example also suggests that referendums on independence tend to be held at times when the international political system is in flux. Allowing referendums on secession—or being forced to accept that a smaller part of a larger empire secedes after a referendum—is not a popular option for the mother country. Accepting that an empire does not have its former power, political influence, and military clout is not welcome and may explain why Indonesia resisted a plebiscite in East Timor for so long. And, of course, the referendum in East Timor was not popular at all in Indonesia, where "Habibie was criticised for allowing the referendum" (Bertrand 2004: 156).

Before looking closer at the statistical support—or otherwise—for the competition proximity model, it is worth considering a theoretically less sophisticated (but perhaps more intuitively convincing) model, namely, that referendums on independence simply tend to occur when there have been changes to the geopolitical system.

Independence Referendums and Geopolitical Upheaval

Very few countries have freely accepted that referendums on independence take place (the exceptions were countries that were under temporary American sovereignty such as the Philippines in 1935 and Micronesia in 1978). But these countries were not part of the American heartland. America may have been one of the first countries to use referendums as a part of the governing process (Delaney and Leitner 1997). However, the use of referendums was not accepted when it threatened the union. As we saw in Chapter 1, some of the Confederate states actually voted to leave the United States. That request was robustly rejected, and the separatist aspirations were dealt with at Gettysburg.

So, generally speaking, and leaving aside the example of Texas and a handful of other confederate states, there seems to be a pattern of sorts here too, namely that referendums on separatism take place in times when an older regime no longer has the power to resist separatist movements. And these conditions generally exist at times when there is a reordering of the balance of power in the international system. Thus, it does not seem to be a coincidence that many referendums on secession or separatism were held in the aftermath of World War II or after the collapse of Soviet communism. An independent Estonia, to mention but one example, is unlikely to have arisen in the absence of the fall of the Berlin Wall.

But a single case study does not prove a general thesis. We are in danger of extrapolating on the basis of a limited set of data. We cannot conclude anything before we have compared this example with other cases. What we need to do to corroborate our hypothesis is to compare all the examples of secessions and determine if the ones that involved referendums took place after momentous changes in the international system. Table 5 lists all secessions in the twentieth century and lists if referendums did or did not take place. (A score of zero is given to countries that did not hold referendums, and a score of one is given in cases when there was a major change in the international system.) We classify three events as major changes: the end of World War I, decolonization, and the fall of communism (limited to these for operational reasons). Based on Table 5 we can categorize the different cases into a two-by-two box.

As Table 6 shows, referendums were held for forty-four of the sixty cases of secession in the twentieth century. Only in sixteen cases was no referendum held. The question is if there is a pattern to these cases. Table 6 clearly suggests that most referendums were held at times of momentous change to the international system.

This pattern seems to be confirmed by Figure 1, which shows the distribution of referendums on separatism. As the figure shows, there is clearly a pattern that these polls have taken place in distinct epochs. But while the figures suggest a pattern consistent with the hypothesis that referendums on separatism are held after momentous international changes, it is difficult to eyeball a complex statistical pattern.

Simple figures tell us relatively little and do not give us a sense of the possible causal connections between momentous political changes and referendums. To get a better sense of the correlations we need more high-powered statistical techniques. The problem here is that we have only categorical variables.

We cannot, therefore, rely on simple regression models. The chi-square method is often applied when comparing two categorical variables and is well suited for testing this hypothesis. While it is not used as much as the regression model, this alternative is arguably better suited for our purposes, not least as we are trying to get an indication rather than a precise figure.

A chi-square test for independence (with Yates continuity correction) indicates a significant association between referendums and momentous changes, $\chi^2(1, N = 60) = 7.253, p = .007$, phi $= -.348$. The statistical calculations suggest that there *is* a positive correlation between secession referendums and seismic changes in the international political system. Furthermore, the calculations of statistical significance show that this relationship is likely to be true in at least 93 percent of the cases.

This, of course, is by no means a perfect relationship (for which we normally require 95 percent). Yet it does indicate that there is some validity

Table 5. Secession Referendums and International Change

Area	Referendum	International change	Year
Norway	1	0	1905
Ireland	0	1	1919
Western Australia	1	0	1933
Philippines	1	0	1935
Iceland	1	1	1944
Cambodia	1	0	1945
Faroe Islands	1	1	1946
Malta	1	1	1955
Togo	1	1	1956
Guinea	1	1	1958
Niger	1	1	1958
Upper Volta	1	1	1958
Sudan	1	1	1958
Gabon	1	1	1958
Senegal	1	1	1958
Ivory Coast	1	1	1958
Madagascar	1	1	1958
Algeria	1	1	1958
Mauritania	1	1	1958
Cameroon	1	1	1958
Singapore	0	0	1962
Malta	1	0	1965
Biafra	0	0	1967
Panama	0	0	1977
Micronesia	1	0	1978
Quebec	1	0	1980
Northern Cyprus	0	0	1983
Palau	1	0	1984
Abkhazia	1	1	1990
Georgia	1	1	1990
Ukraine	1	1	1990
Armenia	1	1	1990
Turkmenistan	1	1	1990
Uzbekistan	1	1	1990
Chechnya	0	1	1990
South Ossetia	0	0	1990
Montenegro	1	0	1992
Western Bosnia	1	1	1992
Serb Kraina	1	1	1992
Slovakia	0	1	1992
Slovenia	1	1	1992
Serb Republic	1	1	1992

Table 5. (continued)

Area	Referendum	International change	Year
Quebec	1	0	1995
Puntland	0	1	1997
Somalia	1	1	2001
Montenegro	1	0	2006
South Sudan	1	0	2011

Sources: Laponce (2010); Pavkovic and Radan (2007).

Table 6. Secession Referendums and Changes in the International Political System

		Fundamental change in the international system		
		No	Yes	Total
Referendum	No	10	6	16
	Yes	11	33	44
Total		21	39	60

Note: χ^2 (1, $N = 60$) = 7.253, $p = .007$, phi = $-.348$.

to the theory. Referendums tend to (but, of course, are not bound to) happen when there are momentous changes in the international system. But this result is a bit banal and trite and suggests that an alternative model, for example, the competition proximity model, should be considered. We now turn to this model.

It should be said at the outset that statistical testing of this model is complicated as such a quantitative model can provide only limited certainly. But assuming—and this is admittedly a big "if"—that we can measure that the initiator is facing competition in the form of a military threat (e.g., as in Bosnia in 1993) or a domestic political threat from the opposition (as in Western Australia in 1933), we can construct a dummy variable (value of 1 if under threat, 0 if no threat). Furthermore, if we use the anecdotal evidence (and, where available, opinion polls), we can develop a quasi-quantitative model that gauges the relative strength of the competition proximity model vis-à-vis the hypothesis that these referendums

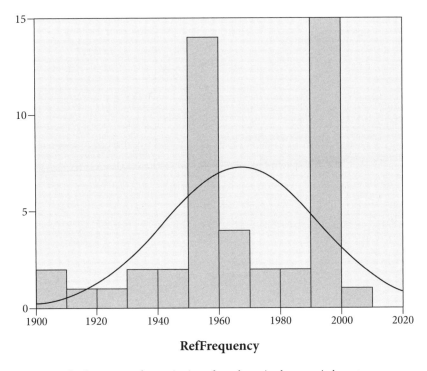

RefFrequency

Figure 1. The frequency of secessionist referendums in the twentieth century.

simply take place after massive geopolitical upheavals. The results of the logistic regression (as the dependent variable is dichotomous) are presented in Table 7.

There is some evidence that the variables for the competition proximity model yield reasonably strong results, though the findings are not as strong as they were for referendums on difference-managing referendums (see the previous chapter). Further, there are outliers and cases that seemingly do not conform to the general pattern. One such outlier is the breakup of Czechoslovakia in 1992. Here "no referendum on the separation, nor the continuation of the common state" took place (Harris 2002: 31) (Box 6). What is perhaps most interesting is that the overall model suggests that referendums on independence are less likely to occur in the wake of geopolitical upheaval. While the evidence is not strong statistically, this is an anomaly that brings into question the pattern reported earlier in this chapter. What seems more certain—though consider the incompleteness of the

Table 7. Competition Proximity Model for Independence Referendums

Variable	Model
Proximity	0.02*
	(0.10)
Competition	0.84***
	(0.80)
International change	−0.86*
	(0.66)
Constant	−0.015*
	(0.53)
N	50
Nagelkerke r^2	.79

Standard errors in parentheses.
Source: Data based on Gallup and IPSOS Mori national polls (http://www.ipsos-mori.com/
Search.aspx?usterms = Elections, accessed December 12, 2012) and case studies of the individual countries cited
in the bibliography.
*Significant at .1.   ***Significant at .01.

data—is that the proxies for competition and support from the median voter once again are statistically significant, although the coefficients are somewhat small. Overall the figures point in the direction of corroboration of the competition proximity model. While all the coefficients are less than one, the competition dummy is statistically significant at the .01 level. Based on the figures, competition—here an external military threat or the threat of electoral defeat—is a strong contributor to the model. The other part of the competition proximity model, however, is less convincing, though it is statistically significant.

From a strictly Popperian point of view, the hypothesis that secession referendums take place only after momentous changes has been falsified, but the hypothesis that referendums on independence take place when the initiators are faced with military competition and have a strong and popular policy has been reasonably corroborated.

From Ballots to Bullets?

The tacit—and perhaps controversial—premise in this book is that referendums can facilitate peaceful transitions from interethnic strife on a territory. The reason for this optimism is not taken out of the blue.

Box 6. A Velvet Divorce Without a Referendum

After the 1992 elections (Václav Klaus on the Czech side and Vladimir Meçiar on the Slovak side), Czechoslovakia broke up. The leaders did not have a mandate for this decision, and the election had not been fought on this theme (Harris 2002: 31). Indeed, opinion polls showed that there was support for continuation of the unified state. However, the two leaders were intent on dividing the state, and both knew that a referendum on the issue would be lost. More than 80 percent of the Czechs and roughly 70 percent of the Slovaks supported federal president Václav Havel's campaign for a referendum (Wolchik 1995: 233). This law was blocked by Slovakian separatists in the Federal Assembly (Innes 2001: 135). And although the "the law on break-up of the federation kept being rejected by the Federal Assembly, eventually a new end of the federation law passed by parliamentary parties to which National Councils adopted recommending resolutions was passed by the Federal Assembly on the second reading on 25 November 1992, after each of the two state legislatures had voted for dissolution of the federation (Harris 2002: 90). How can we reconcile this case? Does it force us to reject the overall conclusion regarding when separatist referendums take place? Not really. The separation took place at the end of a period of international upheaval, that is, the breakdown of communism, and the only reason that a referendum did not take place was due to the fact that opinion polls suggested that a majority was skeptical if not outright hostile toward separation (Wolchik 1995: 233). That the referendum did not take place was not due to a flaw in the theory that such a poll was an anomaly or considered unacceptable. Indeed, Havel, the federal president, called for a referendum and even managed to get signatures supporting a plebiscite from two million voters (Pavkovic and Radan 2007: 73). But the political elites in each of the two would-be states, and especially Meçiar (a socialist) and Klaus (a Thatcherite conservative), knew that their ideological plans could be carried out only if the federation split up. However, it is important to note that separation was not equally supported by both sides. The Czechs—including Klaus's Civic Democratic Party—were opposed to separation and accepted it only after they realized that no other option was available. Conversely, Meçiar's Movement for a Democratic Slovakia demanded international recognition, while the more hard-line Slovak National Party demanded immediate independence. In other words, the "velvet divorce" was above all a demand supported by the Slovakian elite, but not something demanded by the demos or even the ethnos. So why was no referendum held? Perhaps because the two leaders knew that there was very limited support for their policies and because neither of them would face competition if no referendum were held. Using the logic of the competition proximity model, C was small and $(I_m - P_i)^2$ was large.

(continued)

> **Box 6. *(continued)***
>
> ──
>
> The case of the velvet divorce is almost a paradigmatic example of when referendum on an ethnic or national issue is improbable. One may decry the decision not to hold a referendum, and one may argue that the decision was undemocratic and in contravention of democratic norms, but the result was not surprising the light of the competition proximity model.

In Aleksandar Pavkovic and Peter Radan's *Creating New States: Theory and Practice of Secession,* the authors use six case studies, three violent secessions or secession attempts (Biafra, Bangladesh, and Chechnya) and three peaceful ones (Norway, Slovakia, and Québec) (Pavkovic and Radan 2007). The former three all have one thing in common: no referendum was held. Conversely referendums were held in the latter examples. Of course this does not prove that referendums led to peace but it does render this conclusion more plausible.

Relatively few secessions preceded by referendums have resulted in war. For example, when Finland seceded from Russia "the bitter and bloody Finnish civil war left class tensions that Americans can hardly imagine" (Lijphart, Rogowski, and Weaver 1993: 315). But this secession was *not,* as we have seen, the result of a referendum, but occurred perhaps *because* no such vote was held. Had a plebiscite been conducted it would have been clear that there was no support for remaining within the new Soviet Union. (Stalin and Lenin had originally wanted a plebiscite but gave up the idea of one when they realized that support for Finland joining the Soviet Union was very low.)[4]

The fundamental question remains, why do these polls result in a peaceful settlement? And why is it that the absence of a referendum can lead to war? But even more fundamentally, do we, in fact, have statistical evidence that supports the hypothesis that referendums are associated with peace? Table 8 lists all the attempts at secession from 1900 to 2011 and includes dummy variables for whether a referendum was held and for whether war followed the referendum.

As we can see most secessions attempts (whether successful or not) take place after a referendum has been held (73 percent). Of these, 15 percent were followed by the outbreak or continuation of war. Of the thirteen cases where

Table 8. Secession Attempts, 1900–2011

Area	Referendum	War	Year
Norway	1	0	1905
Finland	0	1	1918
Ireland	0	1	1919
Western Australia	1	0	1933
Philippines	1	0	1935
Iceland	1	0	1944
Cambodia	1	0	1945
Faroe Islands	1	0	1946
Malta	1	0	1955
Togo	1	0	1956
Guinea	1	0	1958
Niger	1	0	1958
Upper Volta	1	0	1958
Sudan	1	0	1958
Gabon	1	0	1958
Senegal	1	0	1958
Ivory Coast	1	0	1958
Madagascar	1	0	1958
Algeria	1	1	1958
Mauritania	1	0	1958
Cameroon	1	0	1958
Senegal	1	0	1958
Katanga	0	0	1960
Singapore	0	0	1962
Malta	1	0	1965
Biafra	0	1	1967
Panama	1	0	1977
Micronesia	1	0	1978
Quebec	1	0	1980
Northern Cyprus	1	0	1983
Palau	1	0	1984
Abkhazia	1	1	1990
Georgia	1	1	1990
Ukraine	1	0	1990
Armenia	1	1	1990
Turkmenistan	1	0	1990
Uzbekistan	1	0	1990
Chechnya	0	1	1990
South Ossetia	1	1	1990
Montenegro	1	0	1992
Western Bosnia	1	1	1992
Serb Kraina	1	1	1992

Table 8. (continued)

Area	Referendum	War	Year
Slovakia	0	0	1992
Slovenia	1	1	1992
Serb Republic	1	1	1992
Quebec	1	0	1995
Puntland	0	1	1997
Somaliland	1	0	2001
Montenegro	1	0	2006
South Sudan	1	0	2011

Sources: Laponce (2010); Pavkovic and Radan (2007).

war broke out, seven (56 percent) were preceded by a referendum, namely in Bosnia, in East Timor, and in different parts of Bosnia-Herzegovina.

It is difficult on the basis of these figures to claim that referendums are significantly less likely to result in the outbreak of strife and warfare. But to render this conclusion we can use contingency tables. Using this statistical technique it is possible to calculate a correlation between two ordinary variables, in this case the presence (or not) of a correlation between secession referendums and subsequent wars.

Given that statistical calculations can often be misinterpreted and even abused, there is good reason to take a closer look at these figures. Significance levels demonstrate how likely a result is due to chance. In the present case, the significance level is .99, which suggests that the finding is likely to be true in 99 percent of the cases. The negative relationship between holding referendums and subsequent wars is, therefore, statistically unlikely to be a fluke (Cohen 1988: 79).

Based on this analysis we cannot claim, of course, that the holding of referendums will rule out war, but we can say with some justification that, *statistically speaking*, there is diminished risk that a secession from a state will lead to war if a referendum is held. A phi correlation of $-.43$ suggests a medium to high negative relationship between referendums on independence/secession and subsequent war. However, to meet the requirements of statistical analysis of present-day political science, a more thorough and sophisticated model is required (Table 9). Using logistic regression (a requirement since the dependent variable is dichotomous) we find evidence

Table 9. Logistic Regression Model for Independence Referendums and War

Variable	Model
Negotiation	−2.5***
	(0.61)
Referendum	−1.167*
	(0.89)
Yes vote	−0.07
	(0.80)
Ethnic fractionalization	1.78*
	(1.80)
Constant	1.94*
	(1.3)
N	79
Nagelkerke r^2	.49

Standard errors in parentheses.
Source: Ethnic fractionalization data based on Alesina, Devleeschauwer, Easterly, Kurlat, and Wacziarg (2003).
*Significant at .1.   ***Significant at .01.

of the same pattern, though—as expected—the findings are a bit more nuanced.

The findings also suggest that referendums on secession or independence do not automatically or even predominately lead to war. While it is significant only at the .1 level, the risk of war is negative, with a coefficient of −1.16, though this risk is further reduced if the referendum is preceded by negotiations (coefficient = −2.5, significant at 0.01). Not surprisingly, a higher level of ethnic fractionalization (measured by a negative scale) is correlated with a higher risk of war. While these findings do not amount to solid proof that referendums prevent war, the general tendency is certainly there, and this finding clearly goes against the more alarmist conclusions reached by scholars such as, in particular, Roger Mac Ginty, who—based on case studies but *not* on the basis of aggregate data—suggested that referendums were often correlated with war (Mac Ginty 2003: 3). Of course, here too there are examples of anomalies. While a majority of the referendums held did *not* result in the continuation of wars and hostilities, others did (e.g., in Bosnia in the 1990s). To explain why we cannot rely on *just* statistical patterns but should invoke auxiliary hypotheses. So, is there an auxiliary hypothesis that can account for, say, the war in Bosnia? Looking at the different referendums that have led to war (or have resulted in the continuation of war) there are certain factors and certain common denominators that can be identified. Referendums are more likely to lead to war in cases where there have not been prior negotiations between the parties (Mitchell, Evans, and O'Leary 2009; also confirmed by the regression model above). The case of Northern Ireland is also illustrative. The 1973 Border Poll—which was *not* preceded by negotiations between London and the Sinn Féin resulted in an exacerbation of hostilities. The 1998 referendum, which by contrast was preceded by roundtable negotiations and an agreed outcome, did *not* result in war, and arguably nearly led to the end of violence—apart from a few sporadic outbreaks. Conversely (though it might be to early to tell) the referendum in Southern Sudan in 2011 (held after long negotiations)—while initially leading to more peaceful relations—has not resolved the tensions between the NCP in Khartoum and the SPLA/M in Juba. The jury is still out on the consequences of this referendum.[5]

In addition to this factor, to wit, negotiations prior to the vote, there is another: support from the international community. In Northern Ireland as well as in South Sudan there was international support in the form of mediators from third parties. If we add these auxiliary hypotheses to the general formula, we get the more specified law that "secession referendums do not lead to war if they have been preceded by negotiations between the parties *and* supported by the international community." Because both of these factors existed the referendum in Montenegro in 2006 ostensibly was resolved so amicably (Friis 2007). Conversely, it was precisely because the EU (and in particular the Badinter Commission, named after the French justice who headed the EU's commission) failed to recognize that secessionist referendums must be preceded by negotiations (i.e., that merely voting does not solve the problem) that the war in Bosnia broke out. Bosnian leader Alija Izetbegovic was aware of the problems, but he was prompted by the Badinter Commission to comply with the rules and hold a referendum. Now, it could be argued that the war would also have broken out if Bosnia had seceded without a referendum. That is almost a certainty. But it seems less likely that the war would have broken out if the parties had negotiated and reached an agreement, which could have been submitted to the voters in a plebiscite. But the latter would have taken time, and Izetbegovic was in a hurry. This led to war. If a referendum had been held after negotiations and with the international community as a more or less neutral arbiter, history might well have been very different (Radan 2000: 47). But these caveats notwithstanding, the law that secessionist referendums do not lead to war is at least as strong as the well-known Kantian law that democracies do not go to war against each other (Layne 1994). This is no mean feat for a social science theory!

Conclusion

Referendums on independence have come in waves. Beginning in the 1860s, when several of the Confederate states seceded from the Union in the United States (and hence, perhaps, in part precipitated the Civil War), secessionist referendums were held in, inter alia, Norway (1905), the Philippines (1935), and Western Australia (1933, unsuccessful). However this type of ethnonational referendum became common only after World War II and became almost de rigueur—and possibly even *opinion juris*—in countries seeking independence after the fall of communism. (Only Kosovo's independence in 2011 was not preceded by a referendum, but it ought to be noted that a successful plebiscite was held on the issue in the early 1990s.) Generally speaking, referendums on secession have tended to be held in times of a fundamental shake-up of the international political system. When maps are redrawn, the proposed changes are increasingly required to be legitimized through the active consent of the people in question. This might be a result of greater acceptance of democracy and recognition of the view expressed by Carr (see Chapter 1) that every individual has a right to determine the shape of the political unit to which he or she belongs, which is as great as the right to influence the decision-making process in his or her country (Carr 1942: 39). In recognition of this view, scores of referendums were held in former communist countries after 1989. But the overall best predictor of whether citizens are allowed to vote when a state becomes independent is the competition proximity model. Statistically speaking, the best predictors of whether an independence referendum will be held are political competition and external military threats. If a nationalist movement with popular support is under threat—as, for example, the Baltic states were in the early 1990s—a referendum is a good way to gain legitimacy.

Often these referendums are said to lead to war, but this is not the case statistically speaking. Secession referendums are *not* strongly correlated with war. In fact the causal relationship is the other way round, with a correlation (phi) between secession referendums and peace of − .43 (significant at the .01 level). Of course, referendums alone do not lead to peace.

Box 7. Multioption Referendums: The Cases of Puerto Rico and Newfoundland

Multioption referendums have often been discussed in relation to referendums on ethnic and national issues and polls on independence. For example, there have been relatively high-profile referendums with several options in Sweden, for example, in 1955 when three pension systems were put to a vote and in 1980 when the future of nuclear energy was decided in a three-option referendum. But multi-option referendums have also been discussed in relation to the referendum on ethnic and national issues.

A handful of referendums are particularly interesting in this context: the referendums in Newfoundland in 1948, in Guam in 1982, and in Puerto Rico in 1964, 1993, 1998, and 2012. In all but the last of the Puerto Rican referendums the voters were offered more than one choice: independence, become a state within the United States, and status quo (commonwealth). In two referendums, commonwealth was preferred, but in 1998 "none of the above" received a majority of the votes.

Multioption Referendums in Puerto Rico

Option	1967 (%)	1993 (%)	1998 (%)	2012 (%)
Commonwealth	60.4	48.6	0.1	
Free association			0.3	33.3
U.S. statehood	39.0	46.3	46.5	61.1
Independence	0.6	4.4	2.5	5.6
None of the above			50.3	
Turnout	60.0	74.0	71.0	72.0

Source: Lawrence Leduc (2003); for 2012, Comisión Estatal de Elecciones de Puerto Rico.

Finally, in 2012, in a referendum held at the same time as the U.S. presidential election, 61 percent of the voters voted for statehood and for becoming the fifty-first state. However, it remains to be seen when—or, indeed if—the U.S. Senate will ratify the result. Theoreticians interested in so-called social choice theory have been keen to point out that such multi-option referendums lead

Indeed, there is evidence to suggest that secession referendums are even less likely to lead to war if they are preceded by negotiations and receive support from the international community. This may not be much of a universal law when compared to Newton's second law, but the finding is at least as strong as Kant's famous law of democratic peace.

Box 7. (continued)

to cyclical majorities and no Condorcet winner (options that can defeat all the other options in pair wise contests) (Nurmi 1997). It is beyond the scope of this book to deal with this in detail, but suffice it to say there have been Condorcet winners in three out of four cases.

Newfoundland is another area where multioption referendums have been held. On June 3, 1948, a referendum was held in Newfoundland, at that time a dominion within the United Kingdom. The question was whether the territory should maintain its status (commission government), become a part of Canada (confederation), or become an independent territory with strong links to the United States (responsible government). In the first round of the—very bitter—campaign, the clear winner was responsible government, with 44.6 percent of the votes. Maintaining the status quo dropped out, receiving a mere 14.3 percent. Confederation received 41.1 percent of the total. A second referendum was set for July 22. The confederates, that is, those in favor of becoming a Canadian province, realized that they could win. In order to win additional votes, the confederates adopted two new tactics. First, they decided to emphasize the role played by the Roman Catholic Church in the first referendum (the Church had been staunchly against confederation). In early July the Loyal Orange Association issued a circular letter to all its members. It cited the role played by the Roman Catholic Church, condemned "such efforts at sectional domination," and warned Orangemen of the dangers of such influence, which they should resist. And, in order to win votes from those who had voted for status quo, the confederalists targeted unionist voters and presented the confederal option as a "British Union." The tactic paid off; 52.3 percent voted to become a Canadian province, and 47.7 percent voted for independence. Newfoundland became a Canadian province, and the divisive campaign was soon forgotten. Multi-option referendums are rare—but not unheard of. Whether they are a good idea is debatable, but the fact that the very bitter campaign in Newfoundland in 1948 soon was forgotten probably suggests that they are not as bad as they may seem at first. They are the referendum equivalents of first-past-the-post or the French "second round" electoral systems, for better or for worse (Mitchell 1992).

Box 8. Forced to Be Free? Tokelau's Referendums on Independence

What if the territories in question do not want to sever the ties with their colonial overlords, perhaps for fear of being unable to fend for themselves? New Zealand's prime minister, John Key, took issue with this view that all former colonies should be independent when he questioned the "the accepted wisdom that small states should undergo a de-colonisation process" (speech to New Zealand Institute of International Affairs, April 8, 2008). He had a case in point: the Pacific islands of Tokelau, which are currently under New Zealand sovereignty. Tokelau has its own language and culture but receives most of its annual budget from New Zealand. Had it become independent it would, according to an article about the referendum in the *New Yorker*, have "been the world's second smallest nation after the Vatican." And so far, the territory has not become an independent state. Two referendums have resulted in rejection of self-government, in 2006 (when the majority voted in favor of independence but did not meet the 60 percent supermajority requirement)[6] and 2007 (when another referendum failed by just sixteen votes).[7] Should a third referendum be held? Should the Tokelauans—to abuse Rousseau's term from the *Social Contract*—be "forced to be free"?

Chapter 4

Ethnonational Referendums in Constitutional Law: A Case Study of Scotland

Historically, the question of the legality of self-determination through referendums has, as Philip Goodhart noted, "almost invariably followed national lines" (Goodhart 1971: 107). He continued, "For almost twenty-five years after the Franco-Prussian War the leading French international lawyers, Montluc, Ott, Cabouat, Renan and Audinet steadily argued that the doctrine of self-determination had been established by natural right and international usage. Meanwhile the German lawyers Hotzendorf, Geffker, Stoerk and Francis Liever argued variously that plebiscites were wrong; that they subjected the minority to the rule of simple majority without protection" (111).

Perhaps very little has changed. One of the most persistent and controversial questions regarding national self-determination and the referendums is who is allowed to initiate a vote on independence. Yet for all the justified cynicism, legal issues often constrain the political logic and force actors to make decisions that may not be in their political interest. Scotland is a case in point. In 2011 the Scottish National Party (SNP) won the Scottish Parliament election based on a manifesto commitment to hold a referendum on independence (Tierney 2012: 147). But although the SNP won a majority of the vote, the party was—as a leading constitutional lawyer noted—"clearly aware that it would be democratically perverse, as well as politically and legally impossible, to try to override the legal legitimacy of the [Scotland] Act [1997] by way of an extra-constitutional referendum" (Tierney 2012: 147).

A similar situation occurred in Catalonia, where the separatist party Convergencia i Unió and its allies won an election to the Parlament de Catalunya on a similar pledge in November 2012. To understand how the courts are likely to react, it is illustrative to look at the case study of Scotland to gauge the factors that the courts may take into consideration when ruling on the legality—or otherwise—of a decision to hold a referendum. As all courts—of necessity– are bound by the law of their countries, this analysis is illustrative only and does not provide guidance for how, say, a court in Canada (Webber 1996: 281) or Belgium (De Winter and Dumont 1999) might rule on a similar matter, but for all its limitations a case study may—through "thick description"—provide perspectives that may be relevant and pertinent beyond the single case study (Geertz 1973).

Court Interventions and Votes on National Self-Determination: A Comparative Overview

It is a key part of constitutional politics that the judiciary polices the boundaries of competencies allocated to different actors (Tarr 1997: 1097). In the context of referendums on national self-determination, this has led to several rulings regarding the constitutionality—or otherwise—of decisions by secessionist governments or subunits to hold votes on independence (Oklopcic 2012).

As a general rule, such referendums have resulted in rejections of the decisions to hold referendums on self-determination. For example, in Spain, the Tribunal Constitucional de España, in Judgment 103/2008, held that the Basque Parliament had acted ultra vires and declared the unconstitutionality and subsequent invalidity of the Basque Parliament Law 9/2008 of 27 June (a law on a referendum on de facto independence). This ruling is similar to judgments in the United States and in Canada.

In the United States, the Supreme Court of Alaska ruled in 2006 that a referendum on whether Alaska could seek a legal path to independence was ultra vires—and could not be held (*Kohlhaas v. Alaska* 2006). In reaching this decision, the judges cited the earlier—and much celebrated—case of *White v. Texas* from 1869, in which the Supreme Court held that a unilateral secession would be illegal under U.S. constitutional law (Radan 2006: 187).

In Canada, in a much-cited case, the Royal Supreme Court of Canada held in *Re Quebec* in 1998 that "any attempt to effect the secession of a province from Canada must be undertaken pursuant to the *Constitution of Canada*, or else violate the Canadian legal order" (Radan 2006: 187). From the perspective of Canadian constitutional law, a referendum on the independence would not be permitted due to the absence of a constitutional amendment (Radan 2006: 187).

Based on these cases, it is hardly surprising that opponents of Scottish independence have argued that the vote on independence in 2014 is illegal, as the House of Lords Select Committee on the Constitution did in 2012. Needless to say, the rulings were not as unambiguous as some political practitioners would like to argue. *Re Quebec* was "complex opinion that was far from the unequivocal statement sought by the federal government" (Tierney 2012: 143). And in any case, the issue has now been politically bypassed by the British government, which prudently avoided a legal showdown by granting the Scottish government the right to hold a referendum. But from a theoretical point of view, the issue remains important and raises several questions of interest to other groups seeking to hold referendums on independence.

Would a Referendum on Scottish Independence Be Illegal?

At risk of oversimplifying, Hans Kelsen held that the legal system was pure and the decisions, in principle, could be reached without reference to extra-legal circumstances, such as public opinion or the will or a transient majority (Kelsen 1941).

Politically speaking, it seems self-evident that a manifesto commitment by the SNP (which won the election in 2011) would be sufficient to hold a referendum on independence. But from a "pure" legal point of view, would the Scottish government have this right? Like Spain, the United Kingdom is a unitary state. Under the Act of Union 1707, all power that hitherto resided in the Scottish Parliament (which existed prior to the unification of the two countries) was transferred to the UK Parliament at Westminster. Subsequent to the Act of Union 1707, legislation—even legislation that pertained only to Scotland—was enacted by the Westminster Parliament. This arrangement was subject to the fundamental "bedrock of the British Constitution" (*R [Jackson and Other] v. Attorney General*) that Parliament is supreme and that what "Parliament doth, no authority upon earth can undo" (Dicey 1981: 5).

Box 9. Referendums and International Law

Self-determination after independence referendums is often thought to be a solid part of international law. As Yves Beigbeder—an international lawyer—has noted in a much-cited study, "The crucial requirement for self-determination plebiscites or referenda is the political will or consent of the countries concerned, their conviction that populations should not be treated as mere chattels and pawns in the game, but that their free vote should be the basis for territorial and sovereignty allocations" (Beigbeder 1994: 160). In reality, matters are a bit more complicated. It fact it is a misperception that there is a "right" to secession under international law (Hannum 2011). The issue is complex, and we cannot do justice to the matter in a few paragraphs, but what matters is control over the territory. To state matters briefly, under international law, a country can be regarded as independent when it is recognized by the international community. For this to happen two conditions must—as a general rule—be met. First of all, the people in the territory must express a wish to secede. This was recognized by the International Court of Justice (ICJ) in the *Case Concerning East Timor Portugal v. Australia*) and in the ICJ's similar decision in *Advisory Opinion on Western Sahara*. Second, the country must be in control of its territory. If Scotland or Catalonia were to vote for independence (and if the Scottish or Catalan governments were to be in control of the territory) then the international community would—all things being equal—recognize these new states. But as recently hinted by, there is no obligation to do so. Politics often supersedes international law!

In the late 1990s this position was slightly changed. The Act of Union 1707 was modified by the Scotland Act 1998, which transferred a number of powers to the Scottish Parliament at Holyrood. The exceptions were the "reserved matters" listed in Section 29 and further elaborated in Schedule 5, Paragraph 1 of Part I of the act. The fundamental question from a legal and constitutional point of view is if these reserved matters prohibit a referendum on independence.

Adjudication of Devolution in the Courts

To understand the legal issue it is necessary to look at the wider principles and the relevant case law that may be used to decide the question of the legality of a referendum. Given the wording of the Scotland Act 1998 (see below), there is some ambiguity as to how it might relate to the right of Scotland to hold a referendum to gauge the public's views on independence.

Most legal proceedings relating to the constitutionality of enactments by the Scottish Parliament have been by way of judicial review in the *Scottish Court of Session*. Until 2005, the Scotland Act 1998 granted that certain issues could be heard by the Privy Council.[1] But since the enactment of the Constitutional Reform Act 2005, the judiciary function has passed to the Supreme Court.

While the question of the legality of decisions by the Scottish Parliament was dealt with in relation to compatibility with the Human Rights Act 1998 in *Anderson, Reid and Doherty v. Scottish Ministers* (2001) by the Privy Council, the issues of reserved powers were first considered in *Martin and Miller v. HM Advocate* in 2010.

In *Martin v. HM Advocate*, the Supreme Court was asked to determine if the Scottish Parliament could make changes to criminal law. In that case the Supreme Court established the principle that the legality of acts of the Scottish Parliaments had to "be determined by reference to the purpose of the provision, applying the rule set out in section 29(3)" (*Martin v. HM Advocate* 2010: para. 18, per Lord Hope).

In determining if a decision made by the Scottish Executive or an act passed by the Scottish Parliament was ultra vires, the courts should look at the *purpose* of the Scottish act. If this purpose touches upon a "reserved matter," the act of the Scottish Parliament is acting beyond its constitutionally prescribed powers. In reaching this conclusion, the Supreme Court affirmed Lord Bingham's obiter in *Robinson v. Secretary of State for Northern Ireland* (2002), according to which decisions by devolved parliaments or executives must be interpreted "generously and purposively" (*Robinson v. Secretary of State for Northern Ireland* 2002, per Lord Bingham).

Martin v. HM Advocate also established that in determining the purpose of the act of the Scottish Parliament, the courts should look at "reports to and papers issued by the Scottish Ministers prior to the introduction of the Bill, [and that] explanatory notes to the Bill, the policy memorandum that accompanied it and statements by Ministers during the proceedings in the Scottish Parliament may all be taken into account in this assessment" (*Martin v. HM Advocate* 2010: para. 25, per Lord Hope). *Martin v. HM Advocate* was followed by *AXA General Insurance Ltd v. The Lord Advocate* (2011), in which it was held that while the Scottish Parliament's "democratic mandate to make laws for the people of Scotland is beyond question . . . sovereignty remains with the United Kingdom Parliament. The Scottish Parliament's power to legislate is not unconstrained. It cannot make or unmake any law it wishes" (para. 46). The Supreme Court held that they did *not* "need to resolve the question how . . . conflicting views about the relationship between the rule of law and the sovereignty of the United Kingdom Parliament may be reconciled" as they were dealing with a "legislature that is not sovereign" (para. 51). In other words, decisions by the Scottish Parliament—even if they have been supported by a majority at the ballot box—*cannot* overrule statutes enacted by the Westminster Parliament, as sovereignty resides with the latter.

Interpretation of the Right to Hold a Referendum

How does this relate to the question of the referendum on independence? Not surprisingly the views have tended to reflect party lines and the preferences of the commentators. One of the foremost commentators, the legal scholar, philosopher, and former member of the European Parliament for the SNP, Neil MacCormick, believed that the fundamental position is that under the British Constitution all referendums—as a result of the sovereignty of parliament (Dicey 1981: cix)—are advisory (Bogdanor 1981a: 16). Accordingly, "The Constitution is a reserved matter under the Scotland Act, so how could a Parliament which has no power over the Constitution pose a question about the Constitution and put it to the people? . . . The Scottish Executive has unlimited powers to negotiate with the Westminster government about any issues which could be the subject of a discussion between them, therefore it could seek an advisory referendum" (MacCormick 2000: 725). The rationale for this argument is that neither the enactment of the bill nor the holding of the referendum nor even a vote for independence would end or change the Act of Union 1707 settlement. In terms of legal effects, therefore, independence would be a contingent rather than an automatic effect of a referendum bill, even if we assume that the vote will be for independence.

But this still leaves the question of the purpose of the referendum. While it is possible that it may not have any *legal* effect, Section 29 of the Scotland Act 1998 also states that whether a provision "relates to" a reserved matter "is to be determined . . . by reference to the *purpose* of the provision" (emphasis added).

As we have seen from *Martin v. HM Advocate* and before that—in the context of Northern Ireland—in *Robinson v. Secretary of State for Northern Ireland* (2002), decisions by devolved parliament or executives must be interpreted "purposively" (*Robinson v. Secretary of State for Northern Ireland* 2002), per Lord Bingham). That a decision by the Scottish Parliament to hold a referendum may not have any legal effects is not, therefore, the end of the matter. We must also be able to show that the "purpose" of the act does not "relate to" a reserved matter. But how are we to determine the purpose of the referendum bill?

Those who claim that a referendum would be illegal argue that the "purpose" of any referendum bill would be to further the current Scottish government's aim of achieving independence for Scotland . According to this view, the intended consequence—or purpose—of a referendum is to secure a mandate for negotiating independence for Scotland. The "purpose," therefore, relates directly to a reserved matter, the union of Scotland and England, and is consequently beyond the powers of the Scottish Parliament.

But there is a potential flaw with this argument, namely that it conflates the intention of the Scottish government with the intentions of the Scottish Parliament. While the SNP currently enjoys a majority in the Scottish Parliament, it is perfectly possible that members from other parties may support a referendum for tactical reasons (perhaps because they expect that the vote will be lost and believe that the issue of independence will thereby be removed from the political agenda for a generation). Indeed, this was the explicit position of the former Labour leader Wendy Alexander, and this view has also been supported by the former Conservative secretary of state for Scotland Michael Forsyth. Given that this is a possibility, it would simply not be possible to claim that the majority had a single unitary purpose, namely to end the union. As a result, it cannot be argued that the "purpose" of the legislation relates to a reserved matter.[2]

But the question is if this interpretation is consistent with the position of the courts. In its judgments to date the Supreme Court has *not* looked at the broader intention of a majority in the Scottish Parliament. Rather it has—as we noted above in connection with *Martin v. HM Advocate*—looked at "reports to and papers issued by the Scottish Ministers prior to the introduction of the Bill" (*Martin v. HM Advocate* 2010: para. 25, per

Lord Hope). Based on *Martin v. HM Advocate* it is unlikely that the courts would depart from this principle in the event that they have to rule on the legality of a referendum.

In the present circumstances the purpose of the referendum, according to the Scottish government's consultation paper *Your Scotland, Your Referendum*, is to determine whether there should be additional transfer of power to enable Scotland to become an independent country. This "purpose" would clearly "relate to" a reserved matter under Schedule 5, namely "the Union of the Kingdoms of Scotland and England," and hence it would be "illegal" or "unconstitutional."

In other words, while "the effect" of the referendum may not have legal consequences, the "purpose" of the referendum would relate to a reserved matter, and hence it would be outside the bounds of the Scottish Parliament's constitutional competence.

Democratic Legitimacy or Parliamentary Sovereignty?

But it might be argued that a decision to rule a referendum unconstitutional would run counter to the principles of democratic legitimacy stated in *AXA* and in other previous cases. Indeed, in *R (Countryside Alliance) v. A-G*, it was held that "the democratic process is liable to be subverted if . . . opponents of an Act achieve through the courts what they could not achieve through Parliament" (*R [Countryside Alliance] v. A-G* 2007: para. 45, per Lord Bingham).

Given that the SNP won a majority of the seats in the Scottish Parliament on a manifesto commitment to hold a vote on a referendum on independence, it could be argued that a legal challenge would be exactly this, namely, "achieving through the courts what they could not achieve" through the ballot box.

This argument might be politically persuasive. But it is not legally convincing. From a legal point of view, an "Act of the Scottish Parliament is not law so far as any provision of the Act is outside the legislative competence of the Parliament" (Section 29(1)). Whether a majority of the members of the Scottish Parliament or even a majority of the Scottish people support a particular act is, *legally* speaking, irrelevant. What matters is whether the Act in question has any "effect" on the reserved matters or if the "purpose" of the legislation was to affect the reserved matters listed in

Schedule 5. If so, the legislation, however popular, is void from a legal point of view.

Alternatively, it might be argued that the Scotland Act 1998 does not expressly prohibit a referendum on independence as it was held in *AXA* that "what is not specifically identified as being outside competence is devolved" (*AXA General Insurance Ltd v. The Lord Advocate* 2011: para. 46, per Lord Hope).

It is undoubtedly the case that the Scottish Parliament could hold a referendum on any matter within its competence, for example, on criminal policy, health, or education. However, the question here is not the right to submit issues to the voters on any matter. The question is if the Scottish Parliament is allowed to hold a referendum on a matter that relates to a reserved matter.

How to Interpret Ambiguous Legislation?

The Scotland Act 1998 is, arguably, ambiguous. Given this ambiguity, how are we to interpret the reserved matters? Do they prohibit referendums on independence-related matters? There is a large and varied literature on statutory interpretation, but the British rules are relatively firm and well established (Garrett 2008). Under accepted rules of statutory interpretation of Acts of Parliament in the United Kingdom, the courts may—under the principle established in *Pepper v. Hart* (1993)—use statements by the promoter of legislation if the act is "ambiguous, or obscure or the literal meaning [would lead] to of which leads to an absurdity" (*Pepper [Inspector of Taxes] v. Hart* 1993). While it is debatable whether a literal reading would lead to "absurdity," it certainly would lead to a rather large degree of ambiguity. Hence, we are, arguably, permitted to look at the statement by the minister who promoted the Scotland Act 1998. And doing so resolves the matter. Indeed, in a debate on the Scotland Bill in 1997, the secretary of state—and promoter of the bill—Donald Dewar said (in a response to Mr. Salmond), "A referendum that purported to pave the way for something that was ultra vires is itself ultra vires. . . . Matters relating to reserved matters are also reserved. It would not be competent for the Scottish Parliament to spend money on such a matter in those circumstances" (H.C. Debs 5 December 1998, Col. 257). If the meaning of an ambiguous Act is to be determined by statements by the promoter of the Bill, then it follows that the Westminster Parliament intended that any referendum on independence would be ultra vires. And, as it is a fundamental principle under the British Constitution that Parliament is sovereign, it follows that a decision to hold a referendum that has a purpose contrary to the intention of an act of Parliament would be ultra vires, would be "illegal" and "unconstitutional."

Conclusion

"Legal practice," as Ronald Dworkin once wrote, "is an application of interpretation" (Dworkin 1982: 527). This chapter is an "interpretation," but one based on existing case law. Needless to say, it does not purport to be the final word on the subject. Would a referendum on Scottish independence be legal under the Scotland Act 1998? Legally speaking, the answer depends on whether such a referendum would have any "effect" on, or have the "purpose" of, altering a reserved matter under Schedule 5 of the act.

While it could be argued—as Neil MacCormick has—that an advisory referendum would have no direct legal effects, the courts' interpretation of the word "purpose" is likely to lead to a different outcome. Using the courts' purposive interpretation of legislation—as laid down in *Robinson v. Secretary of State for Northern Ireland* (2002) and in *Martin v. HM Advocate* (2010)—a referendum would be contrary to the Scotland Act 1998. Furthermore, based on the statement by the promoter of the Scotland Act, Donald Dewar, it was clear that he regarded *any* referendum on *any* matter related to independence to be ultra vires.

Chapter 5

Right-Sizing Referendums

It is in general a necessary condition of institutions that the
boundaries of governments should coincide with those of
nationalities.
—Mill (1980: 234)

"Nationalism," George Orwell wrote dismissively, is "the habit of assuming
that human beings can be classified like insects and that whole blocks of
millions or tens of millions of people can be confidently labelled 'good' or
'bad'" (Orwell 1953: 75). Whatever its other possible virtues, the fact
remains that nationalist sentiment creates problems (on virtues, see Miller
1993). In many cases the presence of irredentist groups, whether they
are Tyrol Germans in Italy, German speakers in Belgium, Danes in South
Schleswig, or Muslims in northern India, creates problems that require a
political agreement—or, in extremis, a military solution.

We will leave the military option aside here and focus on political agreements. These are sometimes submitted to voters to decide in referendums.
The method of solving these problems can, to use the terminology of
O'Leary, Lustick, and Callaghy, be described as one of right-sizing borders
(O'Leary, Lustick, and Callaghy 2001). Consequently, the votes on these
issues are "right-sizing" referendums. Such plebiscites are not unknown in
international politics—though, as will be argued below, they have become
rarer than they once were (Anderson 1994). The question is why? In this
chapter we seek to determine when such right-sizing referendums occur.
We do this by testing the hypotheses:

Hypothesis I: Right-sizing referendums tend to occur in the wake of a major conflict or in the wake of changes in the international system.

Hypothesis II: Right-sizing referendums occur for strategic reasons, when the initiator is under political pressure and has a popular cause that will benefit the initiator by submitting to a vote.

Hypothesis I will be contrasted with Donald Horowitz's thesis that such right-sizing occurs when there is a growing ethnic homogeneity of the unit in question (Horowitz 1985: 282).

Our method of resolving this is primarily statistical, using data from all right-sizing referendums held since 1791. Before we can go on to answer this question we need to consider the problem in its context (Quine 1951).

A Brief History of Right-Sizing Referendums

In the ideal world of nationalism, all countries match a people: the Dutch in the Netherlands, the Austrians in Austria, and the Japanese in Japan. Of course, it is never that simple. For a start some of these nations are not as homogeneous as they (or their leaders) would like to think. To resolve these problems we need policies of difference elimination (e.g., genocide or people transferring) or difference management (e.g., federalism, consociational power sharing) or—in extremis—separation (e.g., secession from a larger country or partition of two countries) (McGarry and O'Leary 1994).

But there is another potential problem with the idealized world where the territory matches the populus; sometimes nation-states spill into each other. This, understandably, is not uncommon. Human beings as they are, it is only natural that people meet across borders, get married, and have children—though Margaret Atwood's fictional account in *Surfacing* of the border region between Québec and Ontario tells a different—and rather incredible—story (Howells 2006). Furthermore, borders are state constructs that may result from political negotiations or violent conflict, and sometimes the border from one side does not match up with the border from the other side, as the cases of German speakers in Tyrol shows. Almost everywhere border regions are areas of mixed ethnic groups. This is not always a problem. In some cases these problems have been resolved amicably, but—sadly—in most cases these disputes have led to war and violence.

Have referendums been able to resolve these issues? In some cases, the answer seems to be affirmative. However, not all theoreticians have been enthusiastic about these plebiscites, given their often arbitrary nature. Elie Kedourie dismissed referendums on borders noting that "plebiscites are no more . . . equitable, or less liable to criticism than the traditional methods by which boundaries are determined and which are based on the balance of power and the compromise of conflicting interests" (Kedourie 1960: 126). As will be shown below, Kedourie did not have empirical grounds for his pessimism.

"[Ethnic groups] entertain a subjective belief in their common descent because of similarities of a physical type or of customs or both or because of memories of colonization and migration. . . . It does not matter whether or not an objective blood relationship exists," noted Max Weber (Weber 1978: 389). It is safe to say that ethnonational referendums were predominately right-sizing referendums in areas where groups that entertained what Weber called a "subjective belief" were placed on the wrong side of a border in the first hundred years after 1789.

In the aftermath of the French Revolution several polls were held in areas bordering France as to whether the people living in these territories wanted to become part of France or desired to remain under the sovereignty of their princely or papal overlords, and a handful of referendums were held to determine the sovereignty of smaller areas and dependencies, such as the Ionian Islands and Moldova in the 1850s.

Roughly half a century later the same type of referendums were employed to decide whether areas on the border to the new Italian state should join the newly minted nation (Mattern 1921: 95). After World War I several referendums were held—including one in aforementioned Schleswig—on which country irredentist populations wanted to belong to (Table 10).

After World War II issues not dissimilar to those that occurred in the aftermath of World War I arose. And once again solutions were sought through referendums. This was especially the case in the disputed areas between India and Pakistan.

This use of right-sizing referendums was less pronounced in the next forty years, although there are examples. The Beagle Channel, a narrow strait that runs through the southern tip of South America, had caused quarrels and outright hostilities between Argentina and Chile since the 1880s (Altman 2011: 14). The dispute was finally resolved in 1984, when—

Table 10. Right-Sizing Referendums, 1791–1991

Country	Area	Year	Yes	Turnout
France	Avignon	1791	—	—
France	Savoy	1792	—	—
France	Nice	1792	—	—
Belgium	Wallonia	1793	—	—
France	Moselle	1793	99.3	26.7
France	Mulhouse	1798	98.0	—
France	Geneva	1798	—	—
Italy	Lombard	1848	99.9	85.0
Italy	Regio	1848	90.0	—
Russia	Moldova	1857	99.9	81.0
Italy	Parma	1860	95.0	—
Italy	Sicily	1860	95.0	72.0
Italy	Tuscany	1860	99.8	73.0
Italy	Naples	1860	99.2	80.0
Italy	Marches	1860	95.0	64.0
Italy	Ombrie	1860	95.0	79.0
France	Savoy	1860	95.0	96.0
Britain	Ionian Islands	1863	99.0	—
Italy	Venice	1866	95.0	—
Denmark	Virgin Islands	1868	99.0	—
Italy	Rome	1870	98.0	81.0
Turkey	Kars, Batoumi	1918	79.0	—
Austria	Vorarlberg	1919	80.0	50.0
Finland	Aaland	1919	95.0	—
Germany	North Schleswig	1920	74.0	92.0
Germany	South Schleswig	1920	79.0	91.0
Germany	Allenstein	1920	90.0	88.0
Belgium	Eupen	1920	99.0	—
Germany	Marienwerder	1920	92.0	90.0
Austria	Klagenfurt	1920	59.0	96.0
Germany	Upper Silesia	1921	39.0	97.0
Austria	Tyrol	1921	99.0	—
Austria	Salzburg	1921	99.0	—
Austria	Sophron	1921	65.0	87.0
Germany/France	Saar	1935	90.0	98.0
France	Brigant	1945	90.0	—
Poland	Poland	1946	91.0	88.0
Denmark	Faroe Islands	1946	50.1	64.0
India/Pakistan	Border	1947	57.0	51.0
Italy/France	Brigue	1947	92.0	99.0
United Kingdom	Newfoundland	1948	52.0	88.0
India	Jungadagh	1948	99.0	100.0

Table 10. (continued)

Country	Area	Year	Yes	Turnout
France	Chandernagor	1949	98.0	61.0
International	Saar	1955	32.0	96.0
Ghana	Togoland	1956	98.0	84.0
New Zealand	Western Samoa	1961	86.0	77.0
Cameroon	Bakassi	1961	65.0	89.0
Malaysia	Singapore	1962	71.0	90.0
Somalia	Somalia	1967	60.5	95.4
France	Afars and Issas	1967	95.0	61.0
India	Sikkim	1975	97.0	99.0
United Kingdom	Cocos Islands	1984	88.5	65.0
Argentina	Beagle Channel	1984	82.6	72.4
USSR	Kourilles	1991		
Ireland	Northern Ireland	1998	98.0	54.0
Slovenia	Croatia	2010	51.0	42.0

Sources: Laponce (2010); and Butler and Ranney (1994).

after defeat in the Falklands War—the new civilian president Raúl Alfonsin called a national referendum on November 25, 1984, when the opposition parties had opposed the compromise solution proposed by the Vatican (which had been mediating between the two parties since the late 1970s). Of the Argentine electorate, 82 percent voted to accept the Vatican-mediated compromise. As a result of the vote, the dispute was settled. On November 29, 1984, Argentina and Chile signed a protocol of agreement to a treaty at Vatican City giving the islands to Chile but maritime rights to Argentina. This referendum was a success, according to observers. As a study put it,

> Today, outside the countries involved, few remember the Beagle Channel dispute because it was successfully negotiated to a peaceful solution. The dispute has been recounted in several historical and journalistic works in Argentina and Chile. It has been used generally as a case study to inform discussions of international law, diplomacy, and mediation . . . [scholars] of the conflict, [have] used the dispute to probe theoretical aspects of the goals and effectiveness of mediation. Others too have used the case to illustrate the diplomatic process and the value of long-lasting negotiation in the face of apparent stalemate. (Mirow 2004: 1)

In addition, a decade and a few years later a referendum in the Republic of Ireland on the Good Friday Agreement was held in 1998. Over 90 percent of the Irish voters voted to modify Article 2 of the Irish Constitution, which demanded sovereignty over Northern Ireland (Mansergh 1999).

The most recent example of a right-sizing referendum is the poll held in the former Yugoslavia. On June 6, 2010, a narrow majority, 51.5 percent, of Slovenian voters approved a proposal to bring a border dispute to an international tribunal. The turnout was a mere 42 percent. The referendum was essentially a poll about a tweaking of the borders between the two former Yugoslavian countries. The referendum ostensibly resolved an issue that threatened to delay—or even block—Croatian EU membership.

Having outlined the brief history and use of the right-sizing referendum, we turn to the theory-generating part of this section. In all the cases mentioned, the initiator was under political pressure. Alfonsin was under pressure from the opposition in Argentina, in Northern Ireland the parties that negotiated at Stormond were under pressure from the Democratic Unionist Party and from dissident republicans, and in Slovenia the Socialists (Pozitivna Slovenija) were under pressure from nationalist and bourgeois parties, especially from the conservative opposition party Slovenska Demokratska Stranka. Superficially, at least, it seems that the competition proximity model has considerable explanatory power, but before looking at this model, we need to consider the less sophisticated Hypothesis I.

Is There a Pattern of When Right-Sizing Referendums Occur?

The hypothesis that right-sizing referendums are held after conflicts and after fundamental changes in the international political system is, methodologically speaking, a falsifiable proposition in the Popperian sense, as it is possible to think of referendums that have taken place on border demarcation without a war beforehand.

But, in a sense, we need to go a step further and inquire why a particular group demands that a border be moved and that they join what Inis Claude called a "kin-group" (Claude 1955), that is, a group of "brothers" who live across the border in another jurisdiction. Groups living in border regions are often referred to as irredentist groups (from the Italian word *irredento*,

Table 11. Logistic Regression: Determinants of Right-Sizing Referendums

Variable	Model I	Model II	Model III
Ethnic fractionalization	− 0.07	− 0.51	0.97
	(0.50)	(0.55)	(1.3)
Postwar			0.65
			(0.92)
GDP per capita	0	0	
Year	− 0.109**	− 2.10***	− 0.042*
	(0.65)	(0.071)	(0.023)
System change	2.3**		2.4***
	(1.3)		(0.93)
Constant	212*	412**	
	(127)	(138)	
N	58	58	58
r^2	: .58	: .60	: .43

Standard errors in parentheses.
*Significant at .10.   **Significant at .05.   ***Significant at .01.

meaning "the unredeemed").[1] Traditionally, it has been argued that right-sizing referendums are a result of the presence of such irredentist groups. According to Donald L. Horowitz's much quoted study, "propensity to irredentism is greatly improved as the ethnic homogeneity of the retrieving state increases" (Horowitz 1985: 284). This—though Horowitz does not present it as such—is a classic example of a falsifiable hypothesis. To test this hypothesis and our own competing hypothesis, we can conduct a statistical analysis of factors that seem to be conducive to the holding of right-sizing referendums.

Following Horowitz's thesis, we would expect to find a positive correlation between ethnic fractionalization and the presence of right-sizing referendums. We can test Horowitz's thesis using ethnic fractionalization indices. However, we need to be careful not to overstate our case as the ethnic fractionalization data are somewhat imperfect and, prior to 1960, when most of the right-sizing referendums took place, are rather impressionistic.[2] For present purposes the measures used here are based on the Taylor Ethnic Fractionalization Index. While the coefficients are modestly impressive in Model II and Model III in Table 11, this variable is not statistically significant at the .1 level in any of the models. The hypothesis that ethnic fractionalization is a dominant factor is ipso facto not supported by statistical evidence. This, needless to say, does not mean that we can dismiss the thesis entirely. There may still be some truth to the hypothesis in certain cases and under certain conditions. Indeed, Horowitz's other contention—or auxiliary—hypothesis, that right-sizing policies are also dependent upon the support from the kin group across the border, might explain why the simple model is not statistically supported. Horowitz adds an important caveat to his theory, namely that "if the retrieving group does not have a strong position in the putative irredentist state, its claims will be ignored" (Horowitz 1985: 282).

Where does this leave our own theory, namely that right-sizing referendums occur in the wake of conflict and/or in the aftermath of significant changes in the international system? Statistically speaking, there is no evidence in support of the thesis that referendums on right-sizing policies occur in the wake of wars. The variable—included in Model III—is not statistically significant. This—on reflection—is probably not surprising. Wars follow a different logic, and victors on the battlefield are unlikely to permit their military victories to be challenged by the conquered people in a referendum. Right-sizing referendums may on rare occasions have been held after a conflict. In the case of the aforementioned Beagle Channel referendum, Argentina had recently been at war, but the Falklands War was not with Chile (though General Pinochet supported the British). The Argentineans were forced to hold a referendum because they were weak. The French referendums held in the wake of the French Revolution were somewhat different. These right-sizing plebiscites were held *after* conflict. Indeed, it was French policy to submit annexations to referendums, though these polls were not regarded as fair and free (Mattern 1921: 59).

We have a bit more luck when it comes to the other hypothesis, namely that right-sizing referendums occur after major changes in the international system. As the values for Model I and Model III show, there are positive coefficients (2.3 and 2.4, respectively) for this variable, which in both models are statistically significant at the .05 and .01 levels, respectively. We can therefore conclude—at least statistically—that the hypothesis that right-sizing referendums occur after major system changes is supported by the data. To render this hypothesis plausible, however, we need to look at case studies. (We return to these below in our treatment of the Schleswig Referendums in 1920 and in the border referendums between India and Pakistan.) Again, a bit of historical context is useful.

The world of ethnonational referendums used to be one of right-sizing referendums. For the first hundred years after the French Revolution all but six of the twenty-eight ethnonational referendums concerned the drawing of boundaries and the inclusion (or not) of a country in a neighboring state. But this changed. Since World War II, right-sizing referendums have been rare, as we can see in Table 10. This impression is also confirmed statistically; if we correlate the presence of right-sizing referendums with time, we find that these become rarer the more time progresses. In fact, using Wald measures we find that there is an eightfold decrease in the chance that a right-sizing referendum will be held for every year that passes (significant at .03). The only other factor that is significant is GDP, though only to a limited degree (significant at .9 two-tailed).

Why might this be? One reason could be that the world political system has become frozen in the period after decolonization. Previously referendums were held in countries—especially in Europe—to resolve long-standing disputes. But after these were resolved—in most cases peacefully—the right-sizing referendum became redundant in the West. This is not necessarily the case for the developing world. In Africa there have been several border disputes that one would expect to have been resolved through referendums. For some reason they have not been. This is probably explained by the fact that countries in Africa are keen not to open Pandora's box of ethnic strife. As President Philibert Tsiranana of Madagascar noted at an Organization of African Unity summit as far back as 1963, "It is no longer possible, nor desirable, to modify the boundaries of nations, on the pretext of racial, religious, or linguistic criteria. . . . Indeed, should we take race, religion or language criteria for setting boundaries, a few states in Africa would be blotted out from the map. Leaving demagogy aside, it is not conceivable that one of our individual states would readily consent to be among the victims, for the sake of unity" (quoted in Farley 1986: 16). His colleague, President Keita of Mali, emphasized the same when he noted, "We must take Africa as it is, and we must renounce all territorial claims" (quoted in Farley 1986: 16). It seems that this view of the freezing of borders—often to avoid splits within one's own country—is one of the reasons why there have been fewer right-sizing referendums as time has gone on.

But this explanation is somewhat bland and perhaps even banal. The question is if the more challenging competition proximity model has equal—or even greater—explanatory power. Based on election statistics

Table 12. The Competition Proximity Model and Right-Sizing Referendums

Variable	Model I	Model II
Structural change	−0.21	−0.19
	(0.81)	(0.107)
Competition	0.224*	0.604***
	(0.94)	(0.108)
Proximity	0.10***	
	(.41)	
Constant	−0.38	1.81**
	(0.093)	(0.65)
N	58	58
r^2	.73	.52

*Significant at .10.   **Significant at .05.   ***Significant at .01.
Independent variable Border-changes-with referendum-1, without referendum-0. Period 1945–2010. Source: United Nations Map Library.

and opinion polls at the time of the elections (to measure the level of completion) and based on support for the propositions (as evidenced by support for them at the polls—admittedly not an ideal measure!), the variables for the competition proximity model outperform the postsystemic change dummy when correlated with a dummy variable for referendums or border changes. Furthermore, the r^2 values are greater, .73 and .52, respectively, depending on whether the proximity variable is included in the model. This statistical result is consistent with the case studies that show that political competition and strong support for the initiator's policies often translate into decisions to hold referendums on right-sizing issues.

Cases Studies: The Schleswig Problem

As we saw above (see Table 11), right-sizing referendums have tended to be held in the wake of major changes to the international system. However, to render this statistical pattern plausible we need to ground it in more qualitative evidence. Political science is not just about finding quantitative patterns; it is also about supporting these with historical facts, narratives, and empirical illustrations. In order to render Hypothesis I plausible we look at two examples, the referendums in Schleswig in 1920 and the referendums in India in the late 1940s.

The Danish town of Åbenrå (in German, Apenrade), just north of the border with Germany, is more German than the German city of Flensburg (Flensborg), just south of the border. In the former, the citizens read the local *Der Nordschleswiger*. South of the border, members of the large Danish irredentist group send their children to the posh school Otto Duborgskolen (which teaches in Danish) and read the newspaper *Flensborg Avis*, a daily tabloid written in Danish. In some cases such intermixing can work. There are no lasting hostilities between the Danes and the Germans in Schleswig today (though in this case it took several wars to get this far!). What resolved the problem was—or so it has been argued—a referendum (Wambaugh 1933: 98). In 1920, in the aftermath of World War I, the Danes and the Germans voted in two designated zones.

Several areas north of the border voted to stay in Germany. However, generally, those in Zone 2 (in the south) voted for Germany and those in Zone 1 (in the north) voted to become part of Denmark. The referendums were organized in accordance with Articles 109 to 114 of the Treaty of Versailles and were monitored by a commission of representatives from France, the United Kingdom, Norway, and Sweden (Whelan 1994).

As we have already seen, the idea that the solution to the Schleswig problem was a referendum had already been suggested in 1866, when Bismarck and the Prussian army defeated the Danes in the Battle of Dybbøl and forced the Danes to retreat beyond the Kongeaaen River just north of the ancient city of Ribe. Article 5 of the Treaty of Prague stipulated that a referendum should be held within six years to give the people of the northern part of Schleswig the possibility of choosing between staying German or not. But as we also saw in Chapter 1, the Germans withdrew from this offer as they realized that support for their annexation of the territory was weaker than anticipated before the war.

What is interesting about the Schleswig plebiscites is that they were held in areas that had been unaffected by World War I and concerned countries that had not been at war with one another. The referendum was not held as a result of a victory on either side, but—at least in part—because there was a window of opportunity that enabled the two countries to resolve a long-standing dispute at a time when there were more pressing concerns. As important, perhaps, was the fact that the decision to hold a referendum was part of an international solution. In the case of the referendums in the wake of World War I—and in the case of the Saarland plebiscite in 1955 and the Beagle Channel referendum in the 1980s—the parties reached an agreement following mediation. This seems to have encouraged the parties to reach an amicable agreement.

The referendums were held in two areas that were defined by the Danes, on the basis of preparatory work by the historian Hans Victor Clausen, who had been one of the Danish delegates at the peace negotiations in Paris in 1919. The voters in Zone 1 had to vote en bloc, that is, as a unit, with the majority deciding. In Zone 2 (in the south) each municipality was to decide whether residents wanted to remain in Germany or not—a procedure that obviously favored the Danes (who had been neutral during World War I) (Ministerium für Bildung 1997). But the issue had not taken up much time at the Versailles Conference, and reports suggest that the Danes and the Germans were interested in resolving the issue amicably (Hoffmann 1992).

The first referendum in Zone 1 on February 10, 1920, resulted in an overwhelming victory for the Danes: 74.9 percent voted to join Denmark rule, 25.1 percent to remain German. (However, it should be noted that there were large German majorities in the towns of Tønder and Højer.)

A few weeks later, the voters in Zone 2 voted overwhelmingly to stay in Germany: 80.2 percent. A Danish majority in this zone was produced only in three small villages on the island of Fohr. Technically speaking this did not mean that the whole of Zone 2 would join Germany. However, for logistical reasons, it was impossible to allocate these three towns within Denmark (their combined population was less than three thousand). As a result, the international monitoring commission (Commission Internationale de Surveillance du Plébiscite Slésvig) decided that the whole of Zone 2 should remain German (Forman 1975: 20). The area was transferred. However, it should be noted that the process was in no way smooth after that.

The Danish King Christian the Tenth initially refused to accept the result and dismissed the center-left government led by Thomas Zahle and appointed M. P. Liebe (a conservative lawyer who was not a member of Parliament) and a number of officers to form a new government. The coup d'état led to revolution-like scenes in Copenhagen, which were solved only when the king—after negotiations with the socialist leader Thorvald Stauning—accepted a call for new elections, In the election parties that accepted the referendum results in Schleswig won a majority (Kaarsted 1968: 44).

Right-Sizing Referendums in India and Pakistan

The partition of India and Pakistan created ethnic tensions. The British— through Earl Mountbatten—had declared that only those states that were close to the Pakistani border should join the Islamic Republic of Pakistan. But the British had no authority, and their views carried little weight. However, Mohammad Mahabat Khanji III, the *naweb* (ruler) of the small princely state Junagadh (which is located in the southwestern corner of Gujarat) declared that he wished to join Pakistan (Noorani 2001).

This led to the immediate declaration of secession from Junagadh of the two smaller states, Mangrol and Babariawad. Hostilities broke out. Junagadh occupied the two states. As a way of resolving the conflict (and to show strength), India called for a plebiscite, arguing that 80 percent of the population was Hindu. This was a classic move, completely expected based on the competition proximity model; India faced competition and was convinced that the people in the area were behind them.

Pakistan agreed to discuss a plebiscite, on the condition that the Indian troops were withdrawn. This was rejected by India (again consistent with the explanation that victories on the battlefield are rarely ratified in referendums—see above). The Nawab and his family fled to Pakistan following clashes with Indian troops. India won. A plebiscite was held in February 1948, the result of which was summarized as follows: "Out of an electorate of 201,457, 190,870 cast their votes. Only 91 voted for Pakistan. Of the 31,434 votes cast in the five princeling areas, only 39 voted for accession to Pakistan. . . . The result would not have been different even if the UN had conducted this plebiscite" (Noorani 2001: 17). This effectively ended any further arguments about the ethnic allegiances of Junagadh.

The issue was equally simple in the case of Sylhet (in present-day Bangladesh), although there have been some criticisms that the vote was administered by the Pakistani army and the election staff were apparently supported by the Muslim League. Overall it was a clear-cut and foregone conclusion. In 1947, following a referendum, almost all of the former Sylhet became a part of East Pakistan (with the exception of Karimagnj, which became part of the Indian state of Assam). A majority voted in favor of being part of East Bengal.[3]

But the situation was far from clear in the case of Kashmir. India dominated two-thirds of the region, Pakistan the remainder. An uprising by the Muslim majority against the Hindu Maharajah triggered a buildup of Indian troops, and India attempted to annex the whole area in 1948. This provoked a war with Pakistan. A UN commission called for the withdrawal of both countries' troops in August 1948. The United Nations brokered a cease-fire in 1949, and a five-member commission made up of Argentina,

Belgium, Columbia, Czechoslovakia, and the United States proposed a referendum to decide Kashmir's future. This poll was to be supervised by the UN Commission for India and Pakistan.[4] Although initially accepting the idea of a plebiscite, the Indians drew up a constitution for Kashmir and declared in 1957 that they no longer accepted the principle of a referendum (Ganguly and Bajpai 1994). The result has been several wars and an armed conflict, costing thousands of lives and leading to "terrorist" attacks in India by Kashmiri secessionists. The Pakistanis have maintained that the issue should be decided by a plebiscite, but the Indians—negotiating from a position of strength—have resisted this (Ganguly and Bajpai 1994: 401). But why? Not, obviously, because of a lack of competition (and, in this case, military threats), but because the Indians knew that the value of was large and—formally speaking—because the overall value of the equation was negative as the referendum would be decided by a majority of Muslims who—presumably—would rather join Pakistan. India's reasons for not holding a referendum are understandable and rational, even if they are anything but honorable.

In the case of Kashmir, the situation is clear. India won on the battlefield—and had no desire to undo their military handiwork. In the other example, Sylhet, the same explanation holds true, but in Junagadh it does not. The reason for the latter is probably that the Indians found themselves in a stronger position and realized that they had more support than they had hitherto thought. But the other explanation might also be that the Indians needed the international legitimacy that a referendum grants.

The overall finding, however, is consistent with the hypothesis that we tested in the statistical section, that right-sizing referendums are held when there are fundamental changes in the international system. The border dispute between India and Pakistan was a result of the end of World War II, as well as consistent with the logic of the competition-proximity model.

Last Thoughts

Referendums on borders are relatively uncommon—or rather, they have become rare. It used to be the case that most ethnonational referendums concerned the drawing of borders. This was certainly the case before World War I. Since then right-sizing referendums have become rare. The reasons for this are manifold. One of the reasons is that borders have become fixed;

after decolonization no country wants to open the floodgates that the possible redrawing of boundaries would entail.

Right-sizing referendums—contrary to what was hypothesized at the beginning of this chapter—do *not* consistently occur in the wake of conflicts. While the French revolutionaries were in favor of submitting annexations to referendums in the conquered areas, this practice has disappeared. This is ostensibly because conquers do not want to see their military endeavors undone by the people. Hence, while referendums have been planned in certain areas in the wake of a military conflict, these plebiscites (e.g., the planned UN poll in Kashmir) have not taken place. But the main reason why these referendums have *not* taken place is that the utility of submitting right-sizing issues to the voters in the individual circumstances has proved to be low from the point of view of the initiator. Like with the other referendums discussed and analyzed in this book, right-sizing referendums tend to occur when the initiator is under political pressure and when he or she perceives the proposed solution to be close to the preference of the median voter. Perhaps surprisingly, right-sizing referendums do not seem to be affected statistically by the ethnic homogeneity of the area in question (as had been hypothesized by Horowitz).

Apart from the positive and *wertfrei* question of when these referendums are held, there is, of course, another question, namely whether they are desirable. Elie Kedourie, as we saw above, thought not. Given their track record and the issues they have solved, there is—despite the cynicism behind the decision to hold referendums—some evidence to suggest that they have had desired effect; that is, they have facilitated peaceful rather than violent solutions. Perhaps it is fitting to conclude this chapter by quoting Sarah Wambaugh, who opined,

> There is . . . no perfect method of establishing national boundaries. The problem is one of alternatives, a choice between methods of varying imperfection. To allow questions of sovereignty to be settled by conquest, or by a group of great powers gathered at a Peace Conference, resorting for their method of determination at one time to strategic considerations, at another to language statistics, or to history, or to geographic or economic criteria—such methods are even less satisfactory to democratic principles. Therefore it seems certain that we shall keep the plebiscite as a tool in the workshop of political science. (Wambaugh 1933: ix)

Chapter 6

Difference-Eliminating Referendums: E Pluribus Unum?

In their work on ethnic politics, John McGarry and Brendan O'Leary introduced the concept of difference-eliminating policies in multiethnic states (McGarry and O'Leary 1993). The idea was that ethnic differences in multiethnic states could be eliminated by strategies that emphasize—indeed insist on—the unity of the *demos*. Through active policies of eliminating ethnic differences, the ruling elite or regime could tailor policies that ensure that the state is undivided and that ethnic differences are politically unimportant, if even recognized at all. As the model has recently been summed up, "John McGarry and Brendan O'Leary suggest a very simple and useful distinction between methods that aim at eliminating differences and methods that manage them. Eliminating differences can be achieved through genocide, ethnic cleansing . . . and integration and/or assimilation" (Cordell and Wolff 2010: 18).

But one of the issues rarely discussed is the mechanisms used to gain legitimacy for such a policy of difference elimination. How does a government convince its voters—and possibly other states—that they are united and undivided? One of the ways is through difference-eliminating referendums. This chapter analyzes why such referendums on homogenizing strategies are held and predicts the conditions under which a regime is likely to resort to referendums in order to legitimize difference-eliminating policies. As we shall see, such votes are most likely to take place in autocratic regimes.

Plebiscitary Acclamation: Carl Schmitt

What characterizes these difference-eliminating referendums is not—as in the case of other referendums—a free choice as such. These referendums are not "people's vetoes" in the traditional sense of constitutional referendums (Dicey 1890). The aim of the referendum is generally to show unity; the result has to be unequivocal and acclamatory. The result of the plebiscite has to prove that there are no—or only very few—divisions in the society; formally speaking, $(I_m - P_i)^2$ is small. Hence, the result has to yield almost 100 percent support for the proposition.

In traditional theories of referendums (e.g., as espoused by A. V. Dicey), this institutional device is seen as a conservative break on radical change. The difference-eliminating referendum is the opposite. It is a vote held to prove that the leader or the regime has universal support. Such referendums have been used by several leaders/governments in different parts of the world to show that their policies enjoy almost universal support. For example, in the wake of World War II a referendum held in Belgium to show support for the return of King Leopold III—was unsuccessful (Morel 1992: 858). A few years later Colonel Nasser in Egypt sought (initially with success) to paper over the differences between the Syrians and the Egyptians in the unity referendum in 1958 on the amalgamation of the two countries under the ideology of pan-Arabism (Peretz 1959: 27).

But why use this tactic? What makes a referendum so suitable for acquiring legitimacy for difference-eliminating strategies? This was a question that exercised the controversial German jurist and political theorist Carl Schmitt, especially in *Volksentscheid und Volksbegehren: Ein Beitrag zur Auslegung der Weimarer Verfassung und zur Lehre von der unmittelbaren Demokratie* (Schmitt 1926).

In a section on the nature of the plebiscite, Schmitt noted that "acclamation is a perennial phenomenon in any political society. No state without a people, and no people without acclamation" (Schmitt 1926: 34). He believed that referendums concerning homogenization could be used to engender almost total support for a regime—though he was, of course, aware that the device could backfire (Schmitt 1932: 94).

He further developed this theory in his more well-known treatise *Legalität und Legitimität*, where he provided a more rounded theoretical argument for the need to ensure universal support for public policies. Arguing against parliamentary systems of government (which by their very nature are divisive, as parties represent different strands of opinions and different factions), Schmitt argued that "the institutions of direct democracy, as an unavoidable consequence of democratic thinking, [are] in a superior position to the so-called indirect democracy of the parliamentary state" (Schmitt 1932: 65). As opposed to parliament—whose powers are but delegated by the people—the people themselves have an inbuilt legitimacy. Hence, the "referendum is always a higher form of decision" (Schmitt 1932: 93) as "plebiscitary legitimacy is the single type of state justification that may be generally acknowledged today as valid" (Schmitt 1932: 64).

This theory is not, as the reader will have noticed, a democratic theory in the sense that it provides the voters or citizens with an opportunity to deliberate. Indeed, the theory is elitist in the sense that the leaders propose the questions to be affirmed by the people. In Schmitt's theory, "authority comes from above [and] confidence comes from below" (Schmitt 1932: 94). That is "the people . . . cannot advise, deliberate or discuss. They cannot govern or administer. They furthermore cannot set norms, but can only sanction norms by consenting to a draft of norms laid before them. Above all they cannot pose a question, but can only answer with a yes and no to a question put before them" (Schmitt 1932: 93).

However, it is one thing to unearth the seeming logic behind a particular use of the referendum; it is quite another to find that this has been used in practice. To render Schmitt's theory plausible we need to show that political leaders actually seek acclamation through referendums when espousing difference-eliminating policies. Only when we have done this can we turn to the more general question of overall patterns. Therefore, we need to show that the logic behind Schmitt's theory actually holds true.

Case Study: The Acclamatory Referendum in the Third Reich

The plebiscitary use of the referendum was—perhaps unsurprisingly—found in Schmitt's own *Vaterland* during the Third Reich, namely in the National Socialists' explicit use of difference-eliminating referendums. In 1933, 1934, and 1936 and in the Anschluss referendum in Austria in 1938,

Hitler and his advisers explicitly sought to prove the unity of the Reich and their near universal support for difference-eliminating policies through referendums. The National Socialists, of course, were not natural supporters of referendums. Indeed, Hitler himself had been—at best—ambivalent about the device. In *Mein Kampf*, he criticized parliamentary democracy and advocated "the truly Germanic democracy characterized by the free election of a leader" (Hitler 1972: 83). In the same breath he specified that under a National Socialist regime there would be "no majority vote on individual questions only the decision of an individual" (Hitler 1972: 83).

Once in power, however, Hitler was persuaded by the merits of the difference-eliminating referendum. The two referendums, held in November 1933 (on the withdrawal from the League of Nations) and August 1934 (on conferring presidential powers to Hitler) were textbook examples of Schmitt's theory of legitimacy by acclamation. In a letter to Dr. Wilhelm Flick, the interior minister, the Führer wrote that he favored the referendum as he, Hitler, was "steeped in the conviction that the authority of the state proceeds from the people and must be ratified by them in a free and secret (*geheimes*) referendum" (Hitler 1934: 751–52). This view chimes with Schmitt's belief that "the people acclaims the leader with whom it is identical" (Schmitt 1926: 34) and is indicative of the authoritarian nature of Schmitt's thinking, though, is not necessarily an indication that the National Socialists were influenced by the thinking of a man who was himself a member of the Nazi Party.[1] Schmitt's theory of the referendum as a legitimating device hinges on the result being a resounding and nearly unanimous positive verdict of the people. Such a result was achieved in the referendum in November 1933, when a staggering 95 percent of the voters voted for withdrawal from the League of Nations and rearmament, on a 96 percent turnout (*Wirtschaft und Statistik* 1934: 684).

Needless to say such levels of endorsement should be taken with a degree of caution when they take place in an authoritarian (or even totalitarian) regime. The vote certainly fell short of the present-day standards of a free and fair referendum, and the outcome was anything other than a fair representation of the voters' preferences. Victor Klemperer—the famous diarist—noted that "no one will dare *not* to vote, and no one with respond with a No in the vote of confidence. Because 1) nobody believes in the secrecy of the ballot and 2) a No will be taken as a Yes anyway" (Klemperer 1999: 33). And Otmar Jung outlined how the Nazis used intimidation and

Figure 2. Ballot paper from the 1938 Anschluss referendum. The text asks the voter to support the "reunification" (*Wiedervereinigung*) of Austria with the German Reich. Source: Möchli 1994.

gave out free radios so that everybody could be influenced by the propaganda (Jung 1995: 65).

But even this could not secure total support. Indeed, in Hamburg, previously a communist stronghold, the turnout, at 82 percent, was not much lower than the national average (*Wirtschaft und Statistik* 1934: 684). Even these dizzying heights can show the vulnerability of an authoritarian regime. Acclamation means almost unanimity, yet this was hard to get. In the referendum on whether Hitler should be granted presidential (i.e., dictatorial) powers, *only* slightly less than 80 percent voted to confirm Hitler as Führer (*Wirtschaft und Statistik* 1934: 552). This less than unanimous support was ostensibly one of the reasons why the regime changed tactics in the plebiscite on the Anschluss referendum in 1938 (Jung 1995: 66). In 1938, the Nazi regime still opted for a referendum—and clearly still saw the benefits of gaining the acclamation of the voters. But they took no chances. According to Richard J. Evans's authoritative study, the plebiscite was held "amidst massive manipulation and intimidation. A predictable 99.75 per cent of the Austrian voters supported annexation, although probably, to judge at least from Gestapo reports, only a quarter to a third of the Viennese voters were genuinely committed to the idea of union" (Evans 2005: 655).

In any case, the main objective of the difference-eliminating referendum—that of granting the decision an air of legitimacy through a certain degree of political razzmatazz—was met irrespective of the less than universal endorsement of the Anschluss. The referendum did not convince those skeptical of Hitler, but it served the function of solidifying the support of those already converted, a group that ostensibly constituted a majority of the population.

The referendums held on policies to ensure homogenization in Germany in the Third Reich are thus examples of Schmitt's theory in practice, namely that "the people acclaims a leader [Führer], a master with whom the people is identical and 'the people says, in other words, amen' to his proposal" (Schmitt 1926: 34). But is this strategy also followed elsewhere?

There is some evidence for a similar rationale behind submitting homogenizing or difference-eliminating strategies to referendums elsewhere. French president Charles de Gaulle consciously used referendums to rally support for his famous "certain idea of France" (*une certaine idée de la France*),[2] which sought to strengthen the belief in an undivided and unified nation. (It is no coincidence that the party formed by de Gaulle was called Rassemblement du Peuple Français—Rally of the French People.)

The same Schmittean rationale for holding referendums can be observed in Egypt under Nasser. The 1958 referendum on amalgamating Syria and Egypt into the United Arab Republic (Al-Gumhuriyah al-Arabiyah) in many ways provides an archetypical example of a difference-eliminating referendum. In the words of a contemporary observer, "In Egypt 99.99 per cent of the voters supported the Union and Nasir [Nasser] for president. Out of more than six million voters, fewer than 300 voted 'no' in the election. In Syria, where more than 1,300,000 cast ballots, the vote was 99.8 per cent 'yes' on both issues" (Peretz 1959: 25). Furthermore, "the balloting was not only memorable for these figures, but because it was the first time voting was compulsory for men, the first time it was permissible for women" (Peretz 1959: 32–33). "The week of the plebiscite was a gala" (Peretz 1959: 32–33). In other words, the referendum was a celebration, a show of unity.

Schmitt argued that the people cannot deliberate, let alone govern or administer, but can only sanction the decisions by the leader. In short, the people can respond only yes or no (Schmitt 1932: 93). And, like Schmitt—whom Nasser almost certainly never read, let alone knew—the Egyptian leader supported a "democracy" in which rival fractions and political parties had been replaced by a single individual who, in a manner of speaking, personified the nation.

But difference-eliminating referendums can also go wrong; this is illustrated by this case study from the largest referendum ever held, the 1991 all-Soviet Referendum.

The All Soviet Referendum in 1991: A Case Study of an Unsuccessful Difference-Eliminating Referendum?

The aim of difference-eliminating referendums is to legitimate decisions that paper over deep-seated differences. Yet, like all decisions that involve the people (or in this case the *peoples*), such polls can backfire. One did not need to be a political scientist to see this. Indeed, the headline in the *New York Times* said it all: "Soviet Vote Becomes Test of Loyalties" (Schmemann 1991: A1). And indeed, so it was; the poll was a contest between those who believed in a unified, undivided Soviet Union and those who favored a much looser confederate arrangement with a very weak center—or, in some cases (especially in the Baltic republics), no center at all.

The background to the vote is interwoven with the momentous events that took place in the wake of Mikhail Gorbachev's elevation to the post as secretary general of the Communist Party of the Soviet Union (CPSU) in 1985. As a consequence of the policy of glasnost (openness), the various ethnic groups that constituted the vast empire were offered to utilize the proto-federal structures that were established under the 1977 Constitution. Having previously been a rather grandiose-sounding document awash with bombastic rhetoric about self-government and democracy (but with precious little resemblance to the democratic centralist reality of Soviet politics), the Brezhnev Constitution was suddenly recognized as—if not the supreme law of the land—at least something akin to a constitution in the liberal sense, which sets boundaries for the use of power. Gorbachev—while not ready to accept Western principles of pluralism—recognized that a kind of "rule of law" (*Pravovoe gosudarstvo* in Russian) existed and that the party's word was not law as it had hitherto been (Remington 2006).[3]

Yet despite his support for more openness, Gorbachev was not in favor of anything that could dismantle the Soviet state—or even weaken the authority of the Moscow-based center. Glasnost was aimed at economic restructuring (perestroika). It was not aimed at political reform as such. It is easy to forget that the process of liberalization, which led to the 1991 referendum, was anything but a linear progression toward more liberalization, but that is not how it was perceived at the time. The release of political prisoners in the Baltic states in 1986–87 was an example of relaxation of the authoritarianism of the Brezhnev era. Yet Gorbachev—ostensibly pushed by conservative hard-liners—was also the man who ordered the heavy-handed repression of the national movements in

Lithuania in January 1991 (at a time when the world media's focus was on the liberation of Kuwait).

The fact of the matter was that Gorbachev—the liberal darling of the Western media—was also an authoritarian leader who did not want to transfer power to other political parties, let alone preside over the demise of the mighty Soviet empire. Theoretically speaking Gorbachev was involved in what George Tsebelis has called "nested games" (Tsebelis 1990), that is, he was simultaneously fighting on several fronts. Internally, in the CPSU, he was clashing with hard-liners like Yegor Ligachev, who—while not completely hostile to some sort of reform—wanted to slow the pace considerably, and on the other hand reformist members of the Politburo, such as Boris Yeltsin, the mayor of Moscow. In addition to these battles, Gorbachev had—as a result of the liberalization he himself had started—created rivals in the fifteen Soviet republics that constituted the Soviet Union.

To understand why Gorbachev eventually called the 1991 referendum it is important to understand this power struggle, and especially the role of Boris Yeltsin. Having been left for politically dead after he had been sacked as mayor of Moscow, Yeltsin had staged a remarkable comeback, when he was elected to the Congress of the People's Deputies. From this position he was able to gain a seat on the Supreme Soviet and was elected to the post as chairman of the Presidium, in effect president of the Russian Soviet. This new position, which had come about as a result of Gorbachev's own reforms, gave Yeltsin a power base and a degree of legitimacy that Gorbachev did not have. That Yeltsin used his newly won position to support the national aspirations of the Baltic republics created a problem for Gorbachev and was one of the reasons why he decided to call a referendum on a new constitution on March 17, 1991, when the voters were asked, "Do you consider it necessary to maintain the Union of Soviet Socialist Republics as a Renewed Federation of Sovereign States in which the rights of each nation would be fully guaranteed?" (quoted in White and Hill 1996: 157). But what is interesting from our perspective is not merely this tactical use of the referendum but the degree to which Gorbachev sought acclamation. This—perhaps rather surprisingly—was a view that was almost identical with the considerations of Carl Schmitt. According to Schmitt, as we have seen, "The people would acclaim a leader and say, in other words, 'amen' to his proposal" (Schmitt 1926: 34). For this reason "the plebiscitary process is always stronger" (Schmitt 1932: 64). For the plebiscite establishes a momentary *Volkswille*, affirmed on the spot, with a legitimacy that liberalism cannot question since it expresses the immediate and indirect will of different groups of people, but not by the "People" itself.

But we do not need to delve into German political theory to find a theoretical framework for understanding Gorbachev's course of action. Juan Linz similarly concluded that the executive's power derives from having a direct mandate from the people, that the "basic characteristic of presidentialism is the full claim of the president to democratic legitimacy [and that] very often the claim has strong plebiscitary components" (Linz 1994: 6). It was exactly this legitimacy, gained through the "plebiscitary components" and afforded by the referendum, that Gorbachev sought to use.

Gorbachev himself (as opposed to leaders of the Soviet republics and indeed Yeltsin) did not have a popular mandate. He was hampered by the fact that he had not been elected by the 'people but selected by the inner circle of the Politburo. That had sufficed for earlier leaders, but it would not do at a time when the sovereignty of the people had—improbable though it seemed—become the gold standard of legitimacy even after more than seventy years of essentially totalitarian Marxist-Leninist dictatorship.

Gorbachev—though the architect of this process—had lost control of the pace of change, and needed to regain it. The referendum offered a quick fix, and the perhaps the only way of regaining the momentum. Of course, political ideas do not come out of the blue; Gorbachev (or his advisors) had considered the referendum for some time, not least because it had been one of the more prominent proposals by reformists.

Whether Gorbachev himself had thought long and hard about the referendum remains questionable. The instrument never—perhaps for obvious reasons—played much of a role in the years of communist rule, though both Lenin and Stalin had spoken approvingly of the device as a means of exercising the right of self-determination (White and Hill 1996: 153). To be sure, the referendum had been included in the 1936 Stalin Constitution. On paper the most democratic constitution in the world at the time, the Stalin Constitution stated in Article 48 that the Soviet Union Supreme Soviet Presidium could call a national poll (referendum) on its own initiative or on the demand from one of the Union Republics. But no poll was ever demanded, let alone conducted. This changed in the short political thaw after the twentieth Congress of the CPSU in 1956, when Nikita Khrushchev famously reversed the Stalinist orthodoxy.

In the early 1960s ideologues began to toy with the idea of public participation, and the referendum was explicitly mentioned in the 1961 Communist Party Programme as a means of overcoming inertia in progress toward
communism. The referendum was, in other words, explicitly endorsed by
the party hierarchy. Indeed, Khrushchev himself spoke in favor of the
device (for a summary, see White and Hill 1996: 100–103). This association
with Khrushchev—a figure perceived in a positive light by progressives
within the CPSU—endeared reformers (Gorbachev included) to the referendum. Furthermore, the idea of a nationwide poll had been popular
among dissident figures for some time. In 1975 Roy Medvedev—knowing
no doubt that the idea of a referendum was an idle fancy during the Brezhnev years—proposed the use of the device and argued that a referendum
was "a particularly effective form of direct democracy" (Medvedev 1975:
147) that would extend knowledge of civic responsibility. In fact, Medvedev
went further and suggested that there should be "a compulsory referendum
in each republic every five years" (Medvedev 1975: 155).

This credibility of the referendum made it almost ideal for Gorbachev.
The referendum was attractive to Gorbachev because it provided a basis
for outflanking the parliamentarians by claiming that his policies (1) represented the highest democratic aspirations of the CPSU's most idealistic
period and (2) chimed with demands from dissidents. Furthermore,
going directly to the people, the secretary general of the CPSU could
portray himself as the true champion of the people against the perennially
divided and quarrelling parliamentarians who represented many different
shades of opinions. Again the thinking can (paradoxically) be summed
up by Carl Schmitt, who advocated the use of referendums by autocratic—and populist—leaders. The referendum, like no other institution,
created legitimacy for the "plebiscitary legitimacy is the single last
remaining accepted system of justification" (Schmitt 1932: 93) because
"the institutions of direct democracy, as an unavoidable consequence of
democratic thinking, [are] in a superior position to the so-called indirect
democracy of the parliamentary state" (Schmitt 1932: 65). As opposed to
Parliament ("the ordinary lawmaker"), whose powers are but delegated
by the people—the people themselves, through a plebiscite, have an
inbuilt legitimacy: "The ordinary legislature can intrude on the fundamental rights only on the basis of statutory reservation. However, it cannot set them aside. The extraordinary lawmaker [the people], by contrast,
can do both and, leaving aside all other factors, thereby surpasses the

ordinary legislator and is superior to it in a novel way" (Schmitt 1932: 77). As a result of this logic the referendum was very attractive to the beleaguered secretary general.

Furthermore, Gorbachev—committed as he was to a *Rechtsstaat* of sorts—was in the fortunate position that the Brezhnev Constitution, which was constitutionally the highest law of the land, included a clause (Article 5) about referendums for the "further perfection of socialist democracy," which allowed issues to be "submitted to a nationwide discussion and put to a popular vote (referendum)." It was on the basis of this provision that enabling legislation was passed as early as 1987 in the form of the Law on National Discussion of Important Questions of State and Life, and this enabling Act, in turn, provided the legal basis for the adoption, in December 1990, of the Law on Voting by the Whole People (Referendum of the USSR) (White and Hill 1996: 155). Consistent with the ideals of democracy, Article 1 of the act identified the referendum as a "means for the adoption, through voting by the whole people of laws of the USSR."

But there is a snag with even plebiscitary referendums in places where the votes are not tightly controlled by the executive. It would, of course, be wildly inaccurate to claim that the vote that took place in March 1991 was anything like free and fair by any democratic standards, but the situation was such that Gorbachev and his advisors were not able to rig the referendum.

Granted, the nationalist (and explicitly difference-eliminating) slogans like "We will preserve the unity of the State, which is a thousand years old," delivered at prearranged factory meetings, and the control over the state media gave Gorbachev an advantage, but the result was not a foregone conclusion.

The result was a yes vote—76 percent voted yes—on an average turnout of just over 80 percent. By any standards this was a good result; indeed, the percentage who voted for the Good Friday Agreement—widely seen as a benchmark for success—was lower. In fact, in absolute numbers, this was the biggest endorsement of any referendum in history. Overall, the result was initially seen as a victory for Gorbachev (Walker 2003: 23).

But, and this was crucial for the events that followed, there were wide discrepancies in turnout rates in the republics. And Gorbachev had not been "acclaimed"; the voters had not said "amen" to the result, as required under the Schmittian referendum.

In the Baltic states, only the committed turned out to vote. Indeed, the vote in two of the three Baltic republics was held unofficially by the last remaining stalwarts of Soviet communism. Predictably, Gorbachev did win the referendum—and his proposal for a "renewed federation" was especially endorsed in the Central Asian republics. But with 32 million against and with 2.75 million invalid ballots, Gorbachev fell short of a ringing endorsement, which is part and parcel of difference-eliminating referendums. The fact that the proposal was only very narrowly endorsed in Moscow and Leningrad meant that Gorbachev had failed although he had won by a clear majority (*Nezavisimaya Gazeta* 1991: A1).

The aim of the difference-eliminating referendum is unity, and this was precisely what was lacking. Gorbachev, perhaps oblivious to this logic, defiantly signed the document into law on March 20. But the "renewed federation" never came into force. On August 19, just before the new system was to take effect, Gorbachev was put under house arrest by hardliners. A few days later the show had moved on, and Gorbachev was de facto forced to resign his powers to Yeltsin (who had gained extra legitimacy when he had won the Russian presidential election by securing 57 percent of the votes and by beating Gorbachev's preferred candidate Nikolai Ryzhkov (he only got 16 percent). Gorbachev was politically out of business, not least because he was unable to secure endorsement in the difference-eliminating referendum in March 1991.

It seemed almost paradoxical—or perhaps ironic—that the man who had proposed the referendum and fought for its introduction into Soviet politics was himself a victim of not one but two referendums. He who lives by the sword, dies by the sword! Gorbachev resigned his powers after the Ukraine (a republic that had endorsed Gorbachev's proposal by 70 percent) voted to become an independent country by a large margin (90 percent) in December 1991 (Laponce 2010: 42). The inspired—and tactically shrewd—use of the difference-eliminating referendum meant in practice that the poll became difference *enhancing* rather than difference eliminating.

This would probably not have surprised Carl Schmitt, who admitted that "[t]he appeal of the people will always lead to some loss of independence, and even the famous example of the Napoleonic plebiscites shows how precarious and reversible such legitimating devices are" (Schmitt 1932: 94). The referendum in March 1991 is another example of the potential of a difference elimination referendum to backfire.

Table 13. Difference-Eliminating Referendums, Freedom House Scores, and Ethnic Fractionalization, 1950–2000

Country	Year	Yes	Turnout	Ethnic Fractionalization	Freedom House Scores
Congo B	1973	94.5	77.0	0.695	5
Guinea B	1973	99.0	94.0	0.805	6
Ghana	1978	99.9	95.9	0.868	7
Sierra Leone	1978	97.1	96.2	0.769	6
Northern Cyprus (TRNC)	1983	70.2	78.3	0.2	4
Zaire	1984	99.9	99.9	0.904	6
Togo	1979	99.9	99.9	0.743	7
Congo B	1979	91.1		0.684	7
Morocco	1984	99.0	99.0	0.47	4
Central African Republic	1986	99.4	99.0	0.8	7
Ivory Coast	1986	100.0	100.0	0.868	6
Niger	1987	99.6		0.748	7
Burundi	1991	89.2	96.2	0.281	7
USSR	1991	76.4	80.0	0.667	5
Sudan	1998	96.7	91.9	0.735	7

Source: Based on content analysis of propositions collected by Centre for Research on Direct Democracy.

Toward a General Pattern of Difference-Eliminating Referendums

But these examples say nothing about when and under which conditions such difference-eliminating plebiscites are held. Leaders and regimes may seek acclamation under many different circumstances, but is there a pattern that suggests when they are most likely to do so? For example, are leaders more likely to seek homogenizing strategies in ethnically divided societies than in relatively homogeneous ones? And is this strategy one that is more likely to be followed in autocratic states rather than in polyarchies? Or are difference-eliminating referendums merely the result of social factors such as low (or high) levels of economic development?

Before we look in detail at these matters it is important to note that difference-eliminating referendums (here defined as polls that involve explicit reference to policies of homogenization) have been relatively rare compared to the other referendums on ethnic and nationalist issues (Table 13).

When are such referendums held? What characterizes them? When do they succeed? And what is the rationale behind them? As we can see from Table 13 many of these plebiscites have taken place in polities with high levels of ethnic fractionalization and low levels of democratization (high Freedom House scores), but to reach conclusions we need a formal analysis and to contrast our findings with other possible background variables.

Research Design for Empirical Analysis

What we have seen so far in this chapter is that some referendums have followed the logic of Schmitt's acclamatory referendum; that is, governments in Nazi Germany and in Egypt and Syria under Nasser used the referendum to ensure almost total backing for policies of ethnic and national homogenization. The same was the intention behind the ill-fated All Soviet Referendum in 1991.

One of the premises behind the present book is that social science phenomena can be studied using the methodological approach espoused by falsificationists like Karl Popper (see Chapter 1). This implies that we should be able to develop law-like statements about relationships in the political world of the form "If x then y, x, therefore y."

So when have difference-eliminating referendums occurred? Focusing on the period after 1973—the years for which we have comprehensive data—we can divide referendums on ethnic issues into two categories: difference-eliminating referendums and non-difference-eliminating referendums. Giving the former the score of 1 and the latter the score of 0, we can use this dichotomized variable as our dependent variable in a logistic regression model. Contrasting the dependent variable with a number of different independent variables—and using logistic regression models—we get a number of highly interesting results (Table 14).

The factors we particularly want to test are whether difference-eliminating referendums occur more frequently in ethnically divided societies, whether the level of social and economic development is important, and whether level of democratization is important. One of the fundamental hypotheses behind this study is that the latter is likely to be an important factor, or, put differently, we expect—we hypothesize—that there is a negative correlation between a high level of democratization and a high frequency of difference-eliminating referendums.

Table 14. Regression Models of Difference-Eliminating Referendums

Variable	Model I	Model II	Model III
Ethnic fractionalization	0.024	6.34*	0.131
	(0.195)	(4.19)	(0.198)
Effective no. of parties	−0.050		−0.029
	(0.56)		(0.056)
Freedom House score	0.17***	2.08***	0.185***
	(0.030)	(0.821)	(0.030)
GDP per capita	0	0	0
	(0)	(0)	(0)
HDI			0.1
			(0.012)
Constant	−0.178*	−14.441**	−0.382*
	(0.315)	(6.24)	(0.319)
N	59	59	59
r^2	.92	.90[a]	.82

Note: Wald score for Model II: 6.4 (Freedom House score) and 2.2 (ethnic fractionalization).
[a] Nagelkerke r^2.
Standard errors in parentheses.
*Significant at .10   **Significant at .05   ***Significant at .01

The values in Table 14 suggest that there is a strong tendency for difference-eliminating referendums to occur in countries with low levels of democracy. Across all models, the Freedom House variable is statistically significant at the .01 level. This finding is perhaps not surprising given that countries that have held difference-eliminating referendums include polities like Zaire (where Maputo held a plebiscite on homogenization in 1984), Niger (where president Seyni Kountché submitted a new homogenized constitution to the voters in 1987), and Sudan (where an Islamist constitution, which—like a true difference-eliminating referendum—entirely ignored the presence of the Christian and animist south, was submitted to a referendum in 1998) (Nohlen, Krennerich, and Thibaut 1999: 595). That such referendums have been held may be a result of different factors and circumstances, but it is remarkable that none of the fifteen difference-eliminating referendums held after 1973 have been in countries with Freedom House scores of 4 or below. In each of these cases there is a strong sense—though we cannot prove it—that these referendums were held to secure acclamatory legitimacy. This relationship is strong across all models and is not weakened by the inclusion of other variables. Low levels of democratization are so strongly correlated with difference-eliminating referendums that the relationship might explain why the effective number of parties variable (often a proxy for consensus democracy) plays no statistical role whatsoever. We would, perhaps, have expected that a lower number of parties would have been correlated with more difference-eliminating referendums. This does not seem to be the case—perhaps because authoritarian regimes, despite their lack of competitive choices, often have multiparty systems, consisting of approved parties (Schedler 2006). The situation is similar with the economic and social variables. Social factors, such as GDP per capita and the UNDP Human Development Index, are not statistically significant, and the regression coefficients are miniscule and, indeed, nonexistent.

What does this mean? And can we—on the basis of these findings—make predictions as to the probability of when difference-eliminating referendums occur? The answer is yes. One of the features of logistic regression models is that they enable us to calculate odds ratios using so-called Wald scores.[4] These enable us to calculate the probability that an event will occur. Using the odds ratios from Model II, we find that the Wald score is 6.4. This means that the probability that a regime will hold a difference-eliminating referendum increases 6 times for every unit increase in the Freedom House score.[5]

But these referendums do not occur everywhere. It goes without saying that difference-eliminating referendums—as a matter of logic—occur only in countries where there are differences to eliminate. This apparent logic seem to be corroborated, as most of the states that have held difference-managing referendums have high scores on the ethnic Taylor Ethnic Fractionalization Index, for example Zaire (0.904), Côte d'Ivoire (0.868), and the Soviet Union (0.667), though such referendums have also been held in Northern Cyprus (ethnic fractionalization = 0.0291). While statistically significant only at the .1 level, ethnic fractionalization plays a role, and a unit increase in this variable will, ceteris paribus, result in a 2.2 percent increase in the probability of a difference-eliminating referendum being held.

What we can conclude is that difference-eliminating referendums (DER), mathematically speaking, are a function of two factors, a high Ethnic Fractionalization Index (EFI) and a high Freedom House score (FHS), that is, a low level of democratization. Formulaically, the relationship looks like this:

$$DER = f\,(EFI, FHS)$$

Our hypothesis is thus corroborated; difference-eliminating referendums tend to occur in ethnically divided countries with low levels of democratization.

Of course, there are exceptions to the rule, that is, democratic countries in which homogenizing referendums have been held. The Belgium referendum in 1950 is a case in point. The referendum was framed as a plebiscite on unity, a vote to signify that Belgians—whatever their linguistic background—supported the king. The referendum was anything but. A majority of the voters (57 percent) voted no to his return. As 72 percent voted no in the French-speaking areas (Wallonia and Brussels) and as a majority voted for the king in Flanders, the referendum *did* not—as was intended—paper over the ethnic differences. Rather the referendum acerbated them and led to the conclusion in a later report that referendums on the issue should be avoided as referendums "risk provoking deep-seated antagonisms between the [linguistic] communities" (quoted in Morel 1992: 858).

Needless to say, this referendum does not fit the overall pattern that difference-eliminating referendums take place in autocratic states.

Do these examples then falsify the thesis? In the strict sense, yes. To save the thesis in accordance with the Popperian rules, we need an auxiliary hypothesis that is universal. The auxiliary hypothesis—or caveat—could be that such referendums generally are held in countries with high fractionalization scores, but Belgium does not fit this category either. With only two dominant groups, and an ethnic fractionalization score of 0.551, Belgium does not fit the bill, and we need to restrict the universality of our claim to the period after 1973.

After this date *all* difference-eliminating referendums have taken place in authoritarian regimes. With the exception of Northern Cyprus (ethnic fractionalization score = 0.32) and Burundi (ethnic fractionalization score = 0.31) all the referendums of this kind have taken place in countries with an ethnic fractionalization score of more than 0.70. It seems that authoritarian regimes with many competing ethnic groups feel an urge to show universal support by holding plebiscites—an urge that, interestingly, is not present in more monoethnic societies. This is an interesting finding that adds nuance to the growing research into difference-eliminating strategies. The fact that these referendums almost certainly all were rigged and conducted using standards that fell well short of international practice is less

Box 10. A Difference-Eliminating Referendum in Israel?

Another exception to the rule may be the proposed referendum in Israel, which was debated in the Knesset in 2010. Israel is one of the few democratic countries never to have held a referendum. On occasion proposals have been advanced, often on proposals regarding a peace deal with the Palestinians or another of Israel's foes. The passage of the Referendum Act by the Knesset on November 22, 2010, was no exception. But what is remarkable here is not that another referendum proposal was debated or passed by the Israeli legislature; it was the rationale and the logic behind the bill. Proposing that an a fortiori peace deal with the Palestinian Authority had to be put to a referendum among all Israelis if it did not secure the support of 80 of the 120 members of the Knesset, the chairman of the Knesset House Committee said, "Such a vote [referendum] will promote national unity because even opponents will not be able to argue—as they have in the past—that the Knesset's decision is not accurately supported by the majority of the public" (*Harmonia* 2010: 2). Carl Schmitt, as we saw in the previous chapter, argued, "Democracy requires, therefore, first homogeneity and second—if need arises—the elimination or eradication of heterogeneity" (Schmitt 1985: 9). Paradoxical though it may sound, this very idea—developed by an apologist for the Third Reich— forms the basic rationale behind the proposal put forward by the right in the Israeli Knesset.

important. Although elections and referendums in authoritarian regimes are rigged, they seem to serve a function, and seem to confer a certain legitimacy on the regime (Linz 2000: 34). This, of course, does not mean that these states are free, nor that the referendums held there are desirable. Rather, the presence of difference-eliminating referendums in authoritarian regimes supports Michael Oakeshott's observation that "the plebiscite is not a method by which 'mass man' imposes his choices upon his rulers; it is a method for generating a government with unlimited authority to make choices on his behalf. In the plebiscite the 'mass man' achieved release from the burden of individuality he was emphatically told what to choose" (Oakeshott 1991: 380).

Chapter 7

EU Referendums: Nationalism and the Politics of Supranational Integration

Jean Monnet, the founding father of the European Union, was as honest as he was unequivocal about the involvement of citizens in the process of making an "ever closer union." He confessed that he "thought it wrong to consult the people of Europe about the structure of a Community of which they had not practical experience" (Monnet 1978: 367). So why have political elites not heeded the call of the founding father of the European "project"? And why have they been willing to "introduce an additional veto player" (Tsebelis 2002 116; see also Hug 2002)? Given that governments, presumably, "only hold referendums when they expect to win" (Lijphart 1984: 148), it is, as one political scientist put it, a bit of a "puzzle that governments would voluntarily introduce another veto player in the decision-making process" (Hobolt 2006: 157).

This chapter seeks to answer this puzzle using a formal model, which subsequently will be tested. In addition, the chapter analyzes why referendums are won.

When Are Referendums on European Integration Held?

Perhaps surprisingly, there have—with certain notable exceptions in recent years (e.g., Dür and Mateo 2011; Nielsen 2009)—been relatively few studies of why EU referendums have been held.

One of the few exceptions in the standard literature on referendums is Tor Bjørklund's much-cited article "The Demand for Referendum: When

Does It Arise and When Does It Succeed?" (Bjørklund 1982); another example is Laurence Morel's taxonomy of referendums (Morel 2005). These models are presented and subsequently reformulated into a formal model.

According to Bjørklund, referendums are held in order to paper over differences within a multiparty coalition. Thus, the Norwegian coalition government decided to hold a referendum on European Economic Community (EEC) entry in 1972 in order to avoid a split (Bjørklund 1982). This model applies to other cases too. Indeed, the Swedish bourgeois parties followed the same logic when they agreed to disagree over EU membership in 1994 (Ruin 1996). Bjørklund's model, then, is clear: when a coalition is "divided over an important issue . . . [it] may embrace the referendum as a mediating device" (Bjørklund 1982: 248).

The other explanation is provided by Laurence Morel, who—in empirical work—has analyzed what she calls a "politically obligatory referendum" (Morel 2005). The logic of this model is that a political party facing considerable competition feels forced to hold a referendum to show that it acknowledges the views of the voters. For example, the Conservative government of John Major faced considerable competition from the Labour Party in 1996, and opinion polls suggested that the Conservatives—on this issue—were closer to the median voter than was the Labour Party (McAllister and Studlar 2000; Qvortrup 2006). This model can be formalized. Taken as a whole, an actor, i, is likely to benefit from a referendum if there is considerable competition, C, and if the squared distance between the actor's preference point and the preference point of the median voter is small. In other words, as noted several times before,

$$P_{ref} = \sum_{i=1}^{n} \frac{C}{(I_m - P_i)^2}$$

Empirical Testing of the Formal Model

Morel's and Bjørklund's explanations both have intuitive merits. However, they are based on relatively few—and perhaps selective—cases. The question is if we can find an overall pattern. To test the respective hypotheses, we need to operationalize the variables. Bjørklund's model basically states that there is a positive correlation between the number of parties in a coalition and the propensity to submit issues regarding European integration to the voters. This can be measured by the number of parties in the coalition. Consequently, if there is a positive correlation between the effective number of parties in the government over the period in question and the number of referendums, then we can regard the Bjørklund model as partially corroborated.

It is slightly more difficult in the case of Morel's model. But two factors may lend themselves to an explanation: the electoral volatility and support for integration using Eurobarometer data for the years when a referendum was held. Political competition is often analyzed using the Pedersen Index of Volatility, which measures the net changes in voters' party preferences—how many actually change their support from one party to another (Pedersen 1979).

To test the competition in the party system we use the Pedersen score in the general election in the country immediately before the referendum. Of course, it is possible that the time difference between the two events could affect the Pedersen score. However, based on the evidence analyzed here there is no indication that this is the case.

To measure the $(I_m - P_i)^2$ we simply use support for European integration as measured by Eurobarometer in the year of the referendum. Using these variables it is possible to measure the basic components of the competition proximity model. Model I measures all referendums on EU issues, whereas Model II includes only the referendums held since 1990. Both models are based on ordinary least squares (OLS) regression, as we are interested in the size of the majority and not merely the result. (The dependent variable is yes-vote in the referendum.) For example, there is a qualitative difference between a large yes result, such as in several Eastern European countries, and a narrow majority, such as in the Danish *nej* in 1992 and the French *oui* in the same year.

Model I includes all the referendums held on European integration issues (including referendums in Switzerland on closer ties with the EU). Model II includes only referendums actually held in the European Union or accession referendums to the EU. Given that the *N* value is small in the case of the latter, one should be careful not to draw too many conclusions based on the results.

As Table 15 shows, the variables of the competition proximity model are statistically significant in both the models. While the Pedersen Index—the proxy for competition—adds only marginally to the model—this variable is still statistically significant. The strongest variable statistically is

Table 15. Empirical Test of Competition Proximity Model for Referendums on EU Integration (OLS Regression Models)

Variable	Model I	Model II
Parties in government	0.552	0.313
	(0.609)	(0.597)
Support for EU	0.11***	0.96**
	(0.035)	(0.35)
Pedersen volatility	0.04*	0.04**
	(0.02)	(0.02)
Constant	−10.048*	−9.186**
	(4.14)	(3.95)
N	27	18
r^2	.55	.64

Sources: Eurobarometer (1992–2010); Lane and Ersson (2007); annual data section in *European Journal of Political Research* since 1990.
*Significant at .10   **Significant at .05   ***Significant at .01

support for EU—the proxy for $(I_m - P_i)^2$. When analyzing all referendums on European integration in membership countries, this factor is statistically significant at the .001 level, whereas when analyzing only the referendums since 1990 it is significant only at the .05 level. However, this is acceptable and is understandable since $N = 18$ compared to $N = 27$, so this change in the degrees of freedom will have automatic implications for the standard error/t-ratios. The number of parties in the government at the time when the decision to hold a referendum was taken is not statistically significant. Based on this, admittedly crude, model, there is statistical evidence to support the competition proximity hypothesis. Conversely, if we accept that the Bjørklund model can be tested using the effective number of parties in the government (admittedly a big "if"), then it can be concluded that the latter is not corroborated. However, this explanation needs to be further backed up by case studies and persuasive arguments. So does the model work when submitted to more qualitative scrutiny? To answer this question we must look at countries with different political histories and cultures.

The model, it would seem, holds true for Denmark in 1972. The decision to hold a referendum in Denmark in that year bears all the hallmarks of the competition proximity model. The opposition leader, Jens Otto Krag (Social Democrat), was the favorite to succeed the three-party coalition of the Liberals, Conservatives, and Social Liberals (which he eventually did). But Krag's likely majority was threatened by the left of center Socialist People's Party (SF), which campaigned vigorously against the EEC (Nielsen 2012: 45). The SF leader, Axel Larsen, argued in his campaign that Social Democrat voters could "lend their vote" to SF, which would then be able to block the passage of the accession treaty in Parliament. To neutralize this challenge—to neutralize the competition—Krag proposed a referendum. He did this because opinion polls suggested that his position was supported by over 60 percent of the voters (Petersen 1975: 2).

One might argue that this model works equally well in France and Norway in the same years. However, the fourth referendum held in 1972, the referendum in the Republic of Ireland, does not seem to fit the bill. While there was certainly political competition between Fine Gael and Fianna Fail, neither of the parties had a tactical advantage in proposing a referendum as the two main parties position on the subject were nearly identical (O'Mahony 2009). In fact, until the emergence of Sinn Féin as an electoral force in Irish politics (which happened only in the latter part of the first decade of the new millennium), all the main parties in Ireland were prointegration. Where does this fit in? Does it falsify the competition proximity model?

To a degree, it does. But it might be possible to explain this anomaly using the auxiliary hypothesis of constitutional requirements for referendums (which, it should be noted, meets the Popperian criterion of being independently testable) (Kitcher 1982: 46).

Assuming the auxiliary hypothesis constitutional provisions for referendums is acceptable we can amend the model from simply,

$$U_{\text{ref}} = \sum_{i=1}^{n} \frac{C}{(I_m - P_i)^2}$$

by adding constitutional requirements for referendums C_r. Thus we get:

$$U_{\text{ref}} = \sum_{i=1}^{n} \frac{C}{(I_m - P_i)^2} + C_r$$

Only two countries in the European Union have constitutional requirements for referendums. According to the Irish Supreme Court's interpretation of Article 29.4.3 of the Constitution, as confirmed in *Crotty v. An*

Table 16. The Competition Proximity Model and Constitutional Requirements for EU Referendums (OLS Models)

Variable	Model I	Model II
Constitutional requirement	5.552***	5.298***
	(0.99)	(6.038)
Support for EU	0.02	0.96**
	(1.095)	(0.35)
Pedersen volatility	0.002*	0.01*
	(1.7)	(0.02)
Competition	0.709*	
	(1.395)	
Constant	−3.11	−1.365
	(−1.2)	(−0.924)
N	17	17
r^2	.89	.91

Sources: Eurobarometer (1992–2010); Lane and Ersson (2007); annual data section in *European Journal of Political Research* since 1990.
*Significant at .10   **Significant at .05   ***Significant at .01

Taoiseach, changes to the European treaties must be submitted to referendums (MacMillan 2006). The Irish political parties simply do not have a choice.

In Denmark, a similar situation exists. According to the Article 20 of the Constitution a referendum is required for transfer of sovereignty to an international organization if this is not supported by five-sixths of the members of Parliament, although it should be noted that this is not enforced by the courts as the Danish Supreme Court does not recognize itself as a constitutional court (Spiermann 1998). Adding two dummy variables to the model, we get the results reported in Table 16.

The data for the model include only referendums after 1992. As reported in Table 16, the overall fit for the model is considerably stronger, and variables for the competition proximity model are still significant, though only at the .1 level. As expected the dummy variable for constitutional requirements for further integration is statistically significant at the .001 level in both models. This caveat notwithstanding, it is clear from the data that a constitutional requirement for referendums on EU integration increases the explanatory power of the model.

This conclusion is interesting from a political science point of view. The fact that a constitutional provision can alter the behavior of political actors, even when such action is *not* in their own self-interest, is an important finding. But it is also clear from the model that the competition proximity model (which essentially says that referendums are held when it is expedient for the initiator) still has strong explanatory power.

In an aside about the use of referendums in the United Kingdom, British political scientist Dennis Kavanagh concluded that "the referendum had more to do with political expediency than constitutional principle or democracy" (Kavanagh 1996: 60). The same conclusion can be drawn safely for referendums on European integration across the continent. Having established why referendums are held, the question arises, when are they won—or lost?

Voting Behavior in Referendums on Integration

There is substantial research on the determinants of the outcome of EU membership and EU integration referendums. Some scholars have sought to use previous votes as a guide to future referendums (Baimbridge 2007), while others have sought to develop models across cases (Hobolt 2005). But no simple model has emerged. In recent years, formal models have been introduced, but these have generally been complicated and included a host of variables. The model proposed in this section draws on these models and simplifies them to a more basic, statistically stronger, and intuitively more appealing model. Using the methodology and theories of American political scientists who have scrutinized the voting behavior on ballot measures, such as Bowler and Donovan (1998), Hobolt argued that referendums on European integration can be explained as a result of extraneous factors and the voters' perceived proximity to the government's proposed position (Hobolt 2009).

This model—in part—used the much-cited "Franklin Model," developed by Mark Franklin and colleagues, which hypothesized that referendums were like "Second-Order Elections" and were determined by the popularity—or otherwise—of the incumbent (Franklin, Marsh, and McLaren 1994). The present model simplifies earlier models by combining Hobolt's model with earlier—empirically based—generalizations by the present author that found evidence that referendums tend to be lost if the incumbent has been in power for a long time (Qvortrup 2001a) (for a critique of this thesis, see Szczerbiak and Taggart 2004). The model is as follows:

$$No_i = t_p(\alpha_p - \alpha_i)^2$$

Formally speaking, let t_p denote the time the initiating government has been in office, and let $(\alpha_p - \alpha_i)^2$ denote the difference between the preference position of the voter, i, α_i and the preference point of the government α_p. For reasons to be explained shortly, for a voter, i, to vote "yes" in a referendum on European integration, we will expect that $(\alpha_p - \alpha_i)^2$ has a small value, and that a greater value for t_p, *ceteris paribus*, will reduce the propensity to vote yes. The larger the value of t_p and $(\alpha_p - \alpha_i)^2$, the greater the no-vote.

What is the basis for this model? The evidence for the proximity component is almost self-explanatory; voters vote for positions close to their preferences. Of course, there is always the possibility that the voters are ill informed, but this assertion has been challenged and rebutted in recent years. Overall, we have a considerable body of evidence to suggest that voters—though they have imperfect knowledge about the issues—are able to form opinions on the basis of cues and shortcuts. The voters' attitude toward European integration is therefore likely to be a decisive factor (Hobolt 2005).

The hypothesis that time is an important factor may require explanation. The argument is basically that the longer a government has been in office, the less likely it is to convince the voters of the merits of further integration. Inspired by V. O. Key's observation that "to govern is to antagonize" (Key 1968: 30), this writer has argued elsewhere that "governing is never cost-free. All governments break promises, fail to deliver and enact unpopular laws. The number of years in office is often a positive function of the years in office" (Qvortrup 2001a: 192). Does this model stand up to statistical scrutiny? Again, using OLS regression for the same reasons as above, we find that the model has considerable explanatory value and a high level of statistical significance. Time in office has a coefficient of $-.41$ (significant at 0.05) and the proximity component has a coefficient of 0.17 (significant at 0.05) when all referendums are analyzed.

However, as the figures also show, countries in postcommunist Eastern Europe are more likely to vote yes to European membership regardless of how long their government has been in office, a fact that undoubtedly is a result of the perception that membership in the EU protected them from future influence from Russia (Szczerbiak and Taggart 2004: 557). But the overall findings suggest that the factors identified in the model are empirically verifiable and that the more parsimonious model is supported statistically.

Conclusion

Referendums on European integration are held not for idealistic but for tactical purposes. Submitting an issue to a referendum is not based on an idealized commitment to government by the people, but tends to be the result of a party-led political calculation based on an inverse relationship between electoral competition and perceived support for the initiator's policy. To be sure this relationship can be tempered by provisions for mandatory—or constitutionally required—referendums on EU integration. But apart from Ireland (and to a degree Denmark), most countries do not have such requirements. The decision to submit integration issues to referendums is not an irrational act, but a calculated decision to increase electoral support. The individual voter's decision to support European integration is not irrational, nor is it simply a "second order election"—though aspects of this exist. There is empirical support for the assertion that voters actually base their decisions on their support for European integration. But governments find it much harder to convince the electorate of the merits of "an ever closer union" if it has been in office for a long time. Issues matter, but they cannot be seen in isolation. There is evidence to suggest that Europeans are like the American voters studied by V. O. Key: "To be sure, many individual voters act in odd ways indeed; yet in the large the electorate behaves about as rationally and responsibly as we should expect, given the clarity of the alternatives presented to it and the character of the information available to it" (Key 1968: 7).

Chapter 8

Regulation of Ethnonational Referendums: A Comparative Overview

> What the Assembly [in Paris] calls the free and solemn vote of the
> city of Avignon, which before the revolt had 30,000 inhabitants, is
> nothing but the signature of about 1,000 citizens extorted under the
> menace of death, for that only is the actual number of those who,
> together with a horde of brigands established itself in the city after
> the emigration of nobility and the majority of the respectable people,
> from all the commune. The rest was forced to leave.
>
> —Cardinal Rezzonico quoted in Freudenthal (1891: 4)

Cardinal Rezzonico's protest against the alleged (but very plausible) irregu-
larities during the 1791 plebiscite in Avignon is testament to the fact that
elections and referendums have always been marred by claims of fraud and
vote rigging. Perhaps as long as there have been elections and referendums,
there have been attempts to cheat. Some, of course, have been pretty open
about this. Stalin—in a quotation that is likely apocryphal—is often cred-
ited with the statement "what matters is not who votes, but who counts the
votes." Even so, few scholars have paid much attention to the mundane
details of the administrative aspects of voting. The great Spanish political
theorist José Ortega y Gasset noted—in *The Revolt of the Masses*—that "the
state of health of a democracy depends on technical detail . . . all else is
secondary" (Ortega y Gasset 1937: 201). Yet, despite the recognition of that
todo lo demàs es secundario, neither Ortega y Gasset himself nor many of
his colleagues have dealt with the administrative aspect of referendums

(Seyd 1998; Ranney 1981). Indeed, no less an authority than the great Norwegian political scientist Stein Rokkan noted that "given the crucial importance of the organization [of referendums and elections] it is indeed astounding to discover how little serious effort has been invested in the comparative study [of them]" (Rokkan 1970: 166).

To remedy this, the chapter is concerned with these *detalle técnico*. The chapter surveys the best practices on how to organize referendums on ethnic and national issues.[1] This chapter thus differs considerably from the others. Unlike the other chapters, this one is *not* focused on causal determinants, recurrent regularities, or laws of political science. Rather this chapter provides a practical overview for those who want to hold free and fair referendums. The chapter, in other words, is a *tour d'horizon* of the practical and administrative issues pertaining to holding referendums and not an attempt to arrive at grand predictive theories.

At their most fundamental, referendums are intended to give democratic legitimacy to controversial (and often irreversible) decisions on public policy. As these plebiscites on ethnic and national issues are of wideranging consequences—and as strong political, economic, and emotional interests are at stake—it is not surprising that ethnonational referendums have occasionally led to the exacerbation of long-standing conflicts.

The referendums in Northern Ireland (the Border Poll in 1973), the referendums in Croatia and Bosnia-Herzegovina in 1992 and 1993, and the referendum in East Timor in 1999 are but some examples of referendums that resulted in bloodshed and conflict. While the underlying factors cannot be ignored (see Chapters 2–5), the conduct and administration of the poll can be a key factor in ensuring that the referendum is conducted peacefully—and leads to a peaceful outcome. This was seen in the plebiscite in Northern Ireland in 1998 and the 2006 referendum on independence for Montenegro, which, arguably, were peaceful because they were held based on internationally recognized standards (Tierney 2012: 174).

This chapter outlines the major administrative concerns facing those who plan referendums on national and ethnic issues. These include the following:

1. Registration: Who is eligible to vote, and where and how are they to be registered?

2. Voting: Where should voting take place? Should displaced voters and voters living in the diaspora be allowed to vote? And if so, where?

3. How should the regulating authority (the referendum commission) be composed? And who determines its membership?

4. Should there be a special majority requirement in the referendum in recognition of the implications? Should the result stand if it is supported by less than 50 percent of the eligible voters but by a majority of those voting?

5. How should voting take place? How do voters in illiterate societies distinguish between the options?

6. Who should be in charge of the security arrangements around the referendum?

7. Should governments from the seceding territory or from the mother state be allowed to spend money in the campaign?

8. Should there be limits on campaign spending generally? Or should participants' campaign contributions be capped? And if so, how this should be enforced?

9. How should disinformation be dealt with? Should there be sanctions against those who deliberately spread wrongful information about the referendum?

10. Should both sides have equal broadcasting time? And if so, how is this to be enforced?

These are some of the issues that have been debated regarding referendums in the past decades. To understand them, we deal with them in turn. As we will see, there is a bewildering array of regulations pertaining to referendums, but even as all countries are different, and even as peculiar circumstances exist in every referendum, a number of common denominators exist.

Geographic Area of Registration and Voting (Registration)

One of the first problems facing those wishing to organize a referendum is to define the voters—and hence to register them. This is one of the reasons—or perhaps more accurately, one of the excuses—for not holding a referendum on self-determination in Western Sahara, despite a decision by the African Union to hold a referendum in which "the Sahrawi people could exercise their right of self-determination" (Jensen 2005: 32). Despite the establishment of the United Nations Mission for the Referendum in Western Sahara (MINURSU) to carry out the plan, no referendum has been held as Morocco has been able to stall the process by raising the question about the eligible voters (Jensen 2005: 71). As Erik Jensen, the former head of MINURSU, observed, the referendum had not been held due to problems defining the voters: "The referendum planned for Western Sahara resembles a dessert mirage. The elusive issue: who is Sahrawi, who is West Saharan, and who should be entitled to vote [held up the process]" (Jensen 2005: 1).[2]

As we saw in Chapter 3, the referendum in East Timor was characterized by some difficulties in the registration process. To avoid any repetition of this vote it is instructive to summarize the approach used in that referendum. Registration inside and outside East Timor took place during a period of only twenty days, as two hundred registration offices were opened in East Timor as well as in the major cities in Indonesia and elsewhere abroad, including Sydney, Darwin, Perth, Melbourne, Lisbon, Maputo, Macau, and New York, with adjustments made as appropriate. The United Nations, the Australian Electoral Commission, and the International Organization for Migration were responsible for this part of the operation.[3] This method of registration—where the voters have to actively register—has often led to difficulties and to a low registration rate. For example, in 2004 in Burundi, it was decided to postpone the referendum (a poll on managing the differences; see Chapter 4) when only 67 percent of the estimated voters registered. This caused considerable consternation and could, arguably, have been avoided if the Referendum Commission had followed a procedure of "rolling-mobile registration." Coming to the registration office is often cumbersome and costly for voters. A better approach is for the conducting authority to come to the voters. This is the system used in Mexico (though not for referendums, which have been rare in this country). Here the voters, once registered, receive an electronic voting card, which also serves as an ID card. The advantage of this approach is that it eliminates (or minimizes) the risk that some voters vote more than once. The card is scanned at the polling station, and if it has been used previously, the voter is denied the vote. To prevent forgery, nine security features were incorporated into the card's design, making it almost impossible to duplicate or alter. The security features included a bar code, hologram, photograph, and molecular fusion. In using mobile registration, the Mexican Electoral Commission trained and vetted personnel with knowledge of indigenous groups to ensure that they were eligible to register.

Voting

Who is a member of the demos? Are you still a part of the demos if you leave the country, or are you then merely a part of the ethnos? It is questionable whether those living outside a jurisdiction have forfeited their right to vote. Some litigation in Europe suggests as much. For example, in an obiter dictum in *Matthews v. United Kingdom* (1999: para. 64), the European Court of Human Rights found that "persons who are unable to take part in elections because they live outside the jurisdiction . . . have weakened the link between themselves and the jurisdiction," and can consequently not claim a right to vote.

This might justify the exclusion of Montenegrins living in Serbia in the 2006 referendum. Conversely, there are examples of voters in the diaspora being entitled to vote. In both East Timor in 1999 and Eritrea in 1993, voters living outside the country were allowed to vote. However, in these cases this inclusion of expats was, arguably, justified on account of the displacement that took place due to violent conflict. Whatever the justification, in these cases there were several polling stations, as it was the opinion among the organizers that many voters would find it difficult to travel to the polling stations. In East Timor, voters living in Indonesia were entitled to vote. To ensure that the majority of those who wished to vote were given the opportunity to do so, registration offices and polling stations were set up in Jakarta, Yogyakarta, Surabaya, Denpasar, and Ujung Pandang, that is, in areas with an estimated 10,000 or more East Timorese voters.[4] Some had expressed fear that voters in the "motherland" would be less likely to vote against their Indonesian overlords and that the votes would likely be rigged. There is no suggestion that the voters living in these areas were particularly favorably disposed toward the Djakarta rulers, and the vote appears to have been fair and not rigged. In the rest of East Timor, there were seven hundred polling stations.

In Eritrea, UNOVER (the ad hoc UN body set up to monitor the referendum) organized the vote and registration among the estimated 250,000
refugees. A total of 85,000 people voted, but only half of these were residents of Ethiopia. The polling stations were restricted to areas around the
capital. Here 54,000 voted; 98 percent of them voted for independence.[5]
Needless to say, allowing voting in the part from which the voters have the
option of seceding can be costly. The cost of this operation was rumored
to be US$4.50 per voter, though official figures were not released.

Evidence from other countries suggests that voting take place in areas
with more than 20,000 expats. As noted, the issue was debated in Montenegro. In its "Interim Report on the Constitutional Situation of the Federal
Republic of Yugoslavia,"[6] the Venice Commission in 2001 addressed the
issue of voting rights some five years prior to the referendum:

> As regards the right to vote in the referendum, under the referen-
> dum law any citizen of the FRY resident for at least two years in
> Montenegro has this right. It is fully in line with international stan-
> dards that in a federal State each citizen votes in the federated entity
> of his residence, irrespective of the fact of a possible entity citizen-
> ship. This voting rule corresponds to present practice in Montene-
> gro for parliamentary elections and, while there may be arguments
> in favour of allowing all citizens to vote on the question of indepen-
> dence, the right to vote in a referendum should follow the right to
> vote in elections. A different rule would entail a substantial risk of
> double voting since Montenegro citizens resident in Serbia may vote
> in Serbian elections. The Commission therefore fully shares the
> assessment by *ODIHR* that the residency requirement is justified
> in principle, although it seems excessive to require 24 months
> residence.

There is no consensus on the matter, but it would appear that voters living
outside the jurisdiction are not automatically entitled to vote. The demos
and the ethnos are not always congruent.

Composition of the Referendum Commission

In 2005 the conflicting parties in the Sudan reached an agreement on a
referendum on the future of Southern Sudan. One of the trickiest issues at

the talks and in subsequent negotiations was the composition of the referendum commission. The referendum commission was specifically mentioned in the Comprehensive Peace Agreement (CPA). The CPA talked about "an ad hoc commission to monitor and ensure accuracy. Legitimacy and transparency of the referendum as mentioned in the *Machakos Protocol on Self-Determination for the people of South Sudan* which shall also include international experts." Yet the interpretation of this clause almost caused the outbreak of another war in the autumn of 2009; hostilities were resolved only when the leaders of the two parties met in an emergency session in late December 2009. It was agreed the Sudan referendum commission would consist of an equal number of members from each side.[7]

This structure was particularly in line with the Québec Conseil du référendum. This ad hoc body consists of three judges of the Court of Québec. The Conseil has exclusive jurisdiction to hear any judicial proceeding relating to a referendum, and its decisions are final.[8] But this is not the only way of organizing the administration of a referendum.

In New Zealand, three separate bodies administer the electoral system: the Chief Electoral Office of the Ministry of Justice is responsible for conducting general elections, by-elections, and referendums. The Electoral Enrolment Centre is responsible for the continuous enrolment of voters. Finally, the Electoral Commission is an independent statutory body that registers political parties and logos, supervises financial disclosure, allocates election broadcasting time and funds to eligible parties, and conducts public education and information campaigns on electoral matters. This arrangement is rather unusual, although it has worked well.

The international practice is that the commission's members must not be overtly political figures. While they may be nominated by one or another political party, the nominees must come from the "great and the good" and so transcend narrow party politics. For example, in Ireland members of the referendum commission must be former high court judges.

On the question of the proportion of nominees available to each party, one solution, which would encourage the commission to work by consensus, is to require the commission to arrive at its decisions with a qualified majority. A precedent for that is the Burundi Referendum Commission, which requires a 75 percent majority for all its decisions. Another precedent is the RRC in Montenegro, whose membership consists of "equal representation of both options participating in the referendum" (see Article 10 of the Law on the State-Legal Status of the Republic of Montenegro).

The Two Quorums—Turnout Requirement and Approval Requirement

Turnout and quorum requirements are relatively common in referendums on independence and other referendums on ethnic and national issues. The reasons for this are relatively obvious; foremost among them is that, to quote Beogang He, "plebiscites (or referenda) express a decision made once and for all" (He 2002: 67). Given the importance of the vote, it seems reasonable that "if the approval rate of a referendum is too low, it ought to be discredited. A nearly simple majority does not provide sufficient legitimacy" (He 2002: 77).

But it is not always warranted to have a special majority. For example, a special majority requirement may be a mechanism of obstruction. This was arguably the case in the Soviet Union when Gorbachev insisted that "a two-thirds majority should be required for secession in Latvia." This requirement was, arguably, "unreasonable because the Russian population accounted for 34 percent of the Latvians at the time" (He 2002: 77).

A country that currently operates a supermajority is Israel, where a 60 percent majority requirement is needed in the event of Israel giving up occupied territories (see www.haaretz.com/hasen/spages/997608.html, accessed January 3, 2012).

In the Referendum Act passed by the Parliament of Sudan in December 2009, there was a requirement that the turnout had to be higher than 60 percent. But there was *not* a supermajority requirement; a 50 percent plus one would suffice.

It is common (but inaccurate) to cite the Canadian Clarity Act as a precedent for supermajority requirements. As the example is often mentioned, it is instructive to give a brief description on this model. After the 50.58 percent to 49.42 percent result in Québec in 1995, the Canadian House of Commons sought to ensure that a future referendum would not be won by a narrow margin. The Act, however, stops short of recommending a specific majority:

[The House of Commons shall consider] whether, in the circumstances, there has been a clear expression of a will by a clear majority of the population of that province that the province ceases to be part of Canada. Factors for House of Commons to take into account include (2) (a) the size of the majority of valid votes cast in favor of

the secessionist option; (b) the percentage of eligible voters voting
in the referendum; and (c) any other matters or circumstances it
considers to be relevant. (Clarity Act 2000: c. 26, 2 (1)

As will be seen, these conditions are somewhat subjective and open to interpretation. A better example of a supermajority, albeit a small one, was used
in 2006 in Montenegro (a referendum that has become the gold standard
of best practice); the law stipulated that independence be approved if supported by 55 percent of those eligible to vote. The total turnout of the
referendum was 86.5 percent. In all, 55.5 percent voted in favor and 44.5
percent were against breaking the union with Serbia (Krause 2012).

Another example is Saint Kitts and Nevis in the Caribbean. Under the
constitution, Nevis has considerable autonomy and has an island assembly,
a premier, and a deputy governor general. Under certain specified conditions, it may secede from the federation. In June 1996, the Nevis Island
Administration under the Concerned Citizens' Movement of Premier
Vance Amory announced its intention to do so. Secession requires approval
by two-thirds of the assembly's five elected members and by two-thirds of
voters in a referendum (Article 38.1(b)).[9]

After the Nevis Reformation Party blocked the bill of secession, the
premier called for elections for February 24, 1997. Although the elections
produced no change in the composition of the assembly, Premier Amory
pledged to continue his efforts toward Nevis independence. In August 1998,
a referendum on the question of independence for Nevis failed, and Nevis
presently remains in the federation.

A similar mechanism exists in tiny Tokelau, where a self-determination
referendum also failed to reach the required quorum. Yet these examples
are—given the small size of the countries—not likely to establish prece-
dence in the sense of an international norm with the force of international
law.

In most other referendums (e.g., East Timor in 1999, Malta in 1955,
and the referendums on independence for former Soviet states in 1990),
there were no special majority requirements. Special majorities and turnout
requirements were used in Scotland in 1979. The outcome was a rejection
of the proposal for self-government, although a majority had voted in favor.
The result exacerbated antagonisms. The method of voting must be as simple as possible, to allow maximum effective participation.

In summary, a result endorsed by 50 percent of those voting plus one should be accepted, as long as a majority of those eligible (and registered) to vote have cast a ballot. Some people have expressed concern that turnout might be low, which might consequently lead to a vote for secession. Such examples of so-called false majorities are rare (Qvortrup 2000). While turnout is often low in ordinary referendums (on average 10 percent lower than elections), turnout is usually higher in secession referendums than in general elections. Indeed in Québec in 1995, turnout was in excess of 90 percent.

To ensure that false majorities do not occur, authorities can stipulate that a minimum of 50 percent of the eligible voters turn out. Such a system operates in several countries, including Poland, Italy, and Lithuania.

According to an inquiry carried out by the Venice Commission that provided information on thirty-three of the forty-eight member states of the commission, ten of these states have legal provisions setting a minimum threshold of participation of 50 percent of registered voters. The report by the commission states,

A quorum of participation of the majority of the electorate is required in the following states: Bulgaria, Croatia, Italy and Malta (abrogative referendum),[10] Lithuania, Russia and "the Former Yugoslav Republic of Macedonia" (decision-making referendum).[11] In Latvia, the quorum is half the voters who participated in the last election of Parliament and in Azerbaijan; it is only 25% of the registered voters. In Poland and Portugal, if the turnout is not more than 50%, the referendum is *de facto* consultative and non-binding (in Portugal, the quorum is calculated on the basis of the citizens registered at the census).[12]

System of Voting

There have been several ingenious suggestions regarding the system of voting. In South Sudan it was suggested that if the ballot were split in two, one-half for yes to secession and one-half for no and the relevant half were cast in the ballot box, the voting process would be more user-friendly. The suggestion was not implemented, and anecdotal evidence from other countries' independence referendums indicates that voters, even in illiterate societies, are perfectly capable of understanding the different options.

In East Timor, for example, the voters could choose between two options, each represented by the flag of Indonesia (continued unity) or East Timor (secession). The two symbols appeared on the ballot paper.

Referendum Security

In the Eritrean referendum on independence UNOVER was in charge of security, and the local authorities played a secondary role. This resulted in few instances of voter intimidation, but it came at a cost: US$4.5 million.

Conversely, the vote in East Timor was marred by considerable violence (Schulze 2001). The security arrangements were as follows: The Indonesian authorities were to ensure a secure environment in consultation with UN personnel. A number of UN security guards were deployed to ensure the security and safety of electoral administrators and property, but the Indonesian authorities did not cooperate with the UN personnel and in many instances actively hindered their work (Harrington 2007). This notwithstanding, the United Nations was able to supervise the escort of ballot papers and boxes to and from polling sites. The recommendation—indeed the imperative—is that the United Nations (or another relevant body) be given a key role in the security operations pertaining to the vote.

Government Spending

In referendums around the world, legitimate concerns are often raised about the government using public funds to support a favored position. For example, in 1994, the Austrian government spent considerable sums on a pro-EU campaign, but without violating Austrian election and referendum laws (Büthe 1995). The same has been true, more recently, in Spain, where the government is reported to have spent considerable public funds on a (successful) campaign in support of the European Constitution (*El País* 2005).

In other countries—most notably Ireland—similar examples of government spending in support of a proposition have been ruled illegal by the courts. In an often-cited case from Ireland, in 1995 Patricia McKenna, an Irish MEP, argued that the government had breached the Irish Constitution by spending public funds on aspects other than the impartial organization of the process. While the Supreme Court held that "the Government is clearly entitled to spend money in providing information . . . [and that] the Government, as such, is entitled to campaign for the change and the individual members of the Government are entitled either in their personal, party or ministerial capacities to advocate the proposed change," it ruled that the government must stop short of spending public money in favour of one side which has the consequence of being to the detriment of those opposed to the constitutional amendment (*McKenna v. An Taoiseach and Others, Defendants* 1995: para. 46). Although legally nonbinding elsewhere, this judgment has arguably inspired decision makers in other jurisdictions. There is an emerging consensus that it is illegal for governments to spend taxpayers' money on partisan information, or other partisan activities using the state apparatus. It is thus generally to be expected that during the last weeks of the campaign there is a purdah, that is, a period during which any governmental activities that may be construed as potentially benefiting or promoting a specific political party or prospective candidate are halted or suspended.[13]

Campaign Spending

The issue of whether there ought to be a ceiling on campaign expenditure is contentious. Some argue that expenditure ceilings keep costs within manageable limits, ensure that referendums cannot be "bought" by the richer side, and increase public confidence in the result. Others contend that ceilings prevent a truly effective information campaign.

This is not a conclusive debate. Many argue that the outcome of the referendum seems to be driven by other structural factors, such as the economy, the length of tenure of the respective governments, and other factors (Qvortrup 2001a). Some doubt the importance of money in ballot campaigns, though it has been reported that "negative" spending in many cases has been successful (Gerber 1999).[14]

Still, restrictions on expenditures in ballot campaigns are common. In the 1970s, in the run-up to the first Québec referendum on sovereignty association, the provincial Parliament restricted campaign expenditure and mandated that two campaigns be established representing each side of the argument.[15] Québec's Ministry of State for Electoral and Parliamentary Reform, in a 1977 paper, noted that the regulations it had passed were inspired by Great Britain's experience with a referendum in 1975, which it held up as an "invaluable guide," reflecting a "deep-rooted sense of fair play" (Québec Ministry of State for Electoral and Parliamentary Reform 1977: 7).

In the more recent past (1997–2010) the UK Labour government enacted legislation based on the Québec act, namely the Political Parties, Elections and Referendum Act 2001, which also introduced limits on campaign spending, and due to its comprehensiveness, this Act is often cited as a key reference point in debates about referendum regulation internationally.[16] The restrictions on campaign spending are as follows (Sections 117–18):

- Political parties may spend money in proportion to its percentage of votes in the last general election; parties receiving more than 30 percent receive £5 million, those with between 20 and 30 percent receive £4 million, those between 10 and 20 percent receive £3 million, and so on
- For other permitted participants the limit is £0.5 million
- Individuals may not spend more than £10,000
- Designated umbrella organizations may spend a total of £5 million

Following a referendum, all participants are required to submit a very detailed expenditure report to the commission:

- Each individual expense must be itemized
- Reports must be submitted within three months of the referendum, if the permitted participant incurred expenditure of £250,000 or less or within six months of the election if more than £250,000 was spent
- Permitted participants who spent more than £250,000 must submit a statement from an independent auditor with their report

Similar provisions exist in New Zealand under the Citizen Initiated Referenda Act 1993. Under this Act, it is an offense to spend more than $50,000 promoting the petition (at the qualification stage) and to spend more than $50,000 promoting an answer to the referendum.

Disinformation

Information issues are complex both legally and politically. In the democratic context of free speech, the danger of disinformation is real. There is relatively little legislation on this issue:

- The New South Wales Local Government (Elections) Regulation 1998 establishes (Section 109) that "a person must not . . . print, publish or distribute a 'how to vote' card, electoral advertisement, notice, handbill, pamphlet, or card, containing an untrue or incorrect statement intended or likely to mislead or improperly interfere with an elector in or in relation to the casting of his or her vote." However, there has been no litigation over the regulation, and it consequently remains to be seen how it will be enforced.
- The Local Authorities (Conduct of Referendums) (Wales) Regulations 2004 does not deal specifically with the issue, except for allowing local authorities to publish material, which "refute or correct any inaccuracy in material published by a person other than the local authority" (Section 5.3).
- The British Political Parties, Elections and Referendum Act 2001 does not regulate disinformation, nor does the Québec 1978 Referendum Act.

The traditional response to disinformation is to ensure a campaign period that is long enough for false information to be countered and proven wrong. On this count the referendums in Cyprus 2004, for example, were ill served by the very short campaign period (three weeks). Average referendum campaign periods around the world range between one and six months, but the Cyprus campaigns began less than one month before the vote. By most standards, this is insufficient time for debating, refuting, and challenging allegations made by the different campaigns. The Cyprus campaigns were not, however, unique in this respect. The campaign in Slovakia (on EU membership) in 2004 was shorter (only one week!), as were those in Malta and Slovakia (two and three weeks, respectively). The UK Political Parties, Elections and Referendum Act prescribes only twenty-eight days of campaigning.

Moreover, even a long campaign cannot prevent one side from presenting disinformation late in the process. The question is whether legal mechanisms can prevent the dissemination of deliberately false information; precedent is scarce.

Equal Broadcasting Rights

While it is difficult to ensure parity in the quality or biasness of news reports, public broadcasters are generally expected to strike a quantity balance (i.e., print space or airtime) between the contending sides for referendum-related content.

Equality of access was pioneered in the first UK-wide referendum in 1975, when each side was allocated four ten-minute television spots.[17] In the 1979 referendums on Scottish and Welsh devolution, the Independent Broadcasting Authority decided to allocate broadcasting time to political parties (rather than to the two sides). This proved controversial, since three out of four parties favored devolution, and the decision was subsequently successfully challenged (*Wilson v. Independent Broadcasting Authority*).

- In UK referendums now, the two designated yes and no umbrella organizations are allocated equal broadcasting time.[18]
- A similar policy was adopted in Australia in 1999 and in the Québec referendum in 1995. No other countries have adopted such rules.

Conclusion

Administrative matters pertaining to referendums are often given a rather stepmotherly treatment in the literature. This chapter has sought to rectify this by providing a list of best practices in conducting fair referendums

Referendums are controversial undertakings. No matter what results they produce, there is a near certainty that the losing side will cry foul. To minimize the risk of this the following international standards can—at least in part—limit the perceived illegitimacy of the poll. To secure a free and fair referendum the following is necessary:

1. An electoral commission, whether permanent or ad hoc, should be established. The commission should be tasked with overseeing the information effort (e.g., the production and distribution of a voter pamphlet—in consultation with the two sides). Members of the commission should be representatives of neutral bodies, such as the judiciary, the office of the ombudsman, and/or similar figures whose neutrality is beyond dispute.
2. Public broadcasters should strike a fifty-fifty balance between sides (not political parties) and mandate equal time for spokespeople on

television and radio programs. In other words, television stations should give equal time to each side for nonpaid television commercials.

3. No public funds (taxpayers' money) should be spent to endorse or promote one side or the other.

4. Grants of equal size should be provided to both sides in the referendum. (Umbrella organizations should be established for each side, and both should receive equal grants from the government.)

5. All expenditures must be reported, approved, and published by the electoral commission.

6. Voters in the diaspora and displaced voters should be allowed to vote and register, but both should be monitored by an international authority whose neutrality is beyond dispute.

7. There should be no special majority requirements. A 50 percent plus one requirement has sufficed in most referendums. Supermajority requirements have mainly been introduced as a mechanism to prevent a side from winning.

But no matter how perfectly executed such contests are, there are bound to be unexpected and unforeseeable complications and things that few would have considered beforehand. This was the case when a referendum was held in Togoland in Africa in 1956. The question was whether Togoland should become part of the Gold Coast or whether it should become an independent state. The tensions were running high, and the measures used to lure voters to vote either for or against the proposition were manifold. One particular kind of intimidation concerned the Plebiscite Administrator (the UN-appointed body responsible for the conduct of the referendum). The concern was voodoo curses!

The referendum administers, no doubt, were not personally concerned by the prospect of being killed as a result of a curse pronounced by a fetish priest. But they soon realized that many of the prospective voters were rather troubled by the prospect of being killed by Atano, an evil spirit who allegedly was opposed to Togoland joining the Gold Coast (Farley 1986: 127).

The referendum administrators expressed their undoubtedly honest opinion, when they said that they were in "no position to revoke the curse." Yet the predominately British administrators were a pragmatic bunch. Having taken advice from the Foreign and Commonwealth Office, they added an extra clause to the Plebiscite Regulation (under which the referendum was held). Their concern, after all, was not with metaphysical and otherworldly issues, but with running a referendum. The Plebiscite Administrator simply banned curses. Some voters were still concerned. Some reportedly scribbled on the ballot paper, "Please I am afraid to vote because of the oath sworn by T.A. [a fetish priest]."

Eager that the rules be followed, the medicine man was charged with and convicted for having breached the regulation and ordered to pay a fine! Nevertheless, in the end the effect of the curse was deemed negligible. The motion was passed, though turnout in the region where T.A. resided was below the national average (United Nations 1956: 5).

Appendix A: The Question on the Ballot: Does It Matter?

In January 2012 a YouGov poll suggested that 41 percent would vote for Scottish independence if asked the Scottish National Party's preferred question: "Do you agree that Scotland should become an independent country." However, when the alternative question "Do you agree or disagree that Scotland should become an independent country?" was asked only 39 percent would vote yes. And support would plummet to a mere 33 percent when respondents were asked "Should Scotland become an independent country or should it remain part of the United Kingdom?" (*Daily Telegraph*, August 7, 2012). Does the wording of the question in a referendum make a difference? Or are these discrepancies present only in opinion polls where the respondents have a few moments to make up their minds, as opposed to in a referendum where the voters have been subjected to months of debate? This appendix seeks to answer these questions using data from referendums on devolution, independence, and self-government from 1980 to 2011.

There has been considerable debate about the wording of the question on the ballot in referendums on independence, and pundits have expressed different views based on anecdotal evidence. The argument that the wording matters—credibly enough—holds that a biased and one-sided question can prompt the voters to vote yes to a question that they—had they understood it—would have rejected. That biased questions can determine how people answer the question has always been acknowledged by pollsters. Indeed, no less a figure than the pollster George Gallup was one of the first to admit this in his classic article "Question Wording in Public Opinion Polls" (Gallup 1941).

But it does not follow that voters in referendums will react in the same way as those polled in a mass survey. True, in research dating back to the early 1980s, David Magleby hinted that wording might matter if there are many propositions on the ballot at the same time. That is, if the voters read the question for the first time when they enter the polling booth, they might be swayed by emotive language (Magleby 1984). But the same does not necessarily hold true if voters are faced with a single question that has been debated for weeks or even months, as is the case with most referendums outside the United States and Switzerland. In most countries, referendums are held rarely and mainly on controversial issues (Butler and Ranney 1978: 221).

The question is, will voters be swayed by what U.S. President James Madison called "artful misrepresentations" (Madison 1987: 371) in the form of misleading statements on the ballot? Needless to say, there are referendums on many other issues than devolution, self-determination, and independence, for example, on European integration (Hobolt 2009) or on general policy issues (Altman 2011). Yet ethnic and national issues are some of the most emotive and sensitive. We, therefore, have reason to believe that emotive or biased questions in these polls are most likely to have an effect. We can hypothesize that if wording is to have an effect, it is likely to be in these referendums.

Another, and more methodological, reason for focusing on these referendums is that they are homogeneous and enable us to compare like with like by keeping the background variables relatively constant. In other words, by limiting our analysis to this class we satisfy the requirement of what Adam Przeworski has termed "unit homogeneity" (Przeworski 2007: 151). Furthermore, with seventy-four cases, devolution and independence constitutes the largest category of referendums in the period, and provides us with a large N that makes statistical analysis meaningful (Altman 2011).

Last, the issue of national and ethnic politics is exceptionally well researched and has been characterized by extensive theory building in recent years, enabling us to put the findings into context (Connor 1994; Greenfield and Eastwood 2005).

Referendum questions have come in many shapes and sizes, from the bland to the blatantly biased. For example, in Northern Ireland in 1998, the voters were asked to approve (or otherwise) the rather neutral question, "Do you support the agreement reached in multi-party talks on Northern

Ireland and set out in Command Paper 3883?" In all, 71.2 percent did. "Command Paper 3883" was a coded reference to the official document containing the Belfast Agreement on power sharing, but despite the lack of references to the policy contained in the "Command Paper," voters were seemingly aware of the issues (McGarry and O'Leary 2006).

In other referendums, however, the voters were asked more leading questions. For example, in Chile in 1978, the junta asked the voters whether they supported the following statement: "In the face of international aggression against the government of our fatherland, I support President Pinochet in his defence of Chile's dignity, and I once again confirm the legitimacy of the government of the republic in its leadership of the institutional proceedings in this country" (quoted in Butler and Ranney 1994: 5). Not surprisingly, the voters endorsed the proposition (IDEA 2008: 49).

There are several examples of similar questions in referendums on devolution and national self-determination. In 1999, in East Timor, the voters were asked, "Do you *accept* the proposed special autonomy for East Timor within the Unitary State of the Republic of Indonesia?" (emphasis added). A majority of the voters—close to 75 percent—*rejected* the proposal, with the result that East Timor became independent. In this internationally monitored referendum the value-laden word "accept" did not swing the voters (Bertrand 2004). But there are examples of the opposite. In Spain, in Andalusia, in 1980, the voters were asked, "Do you give your *agreement* to the ratification of the initiative, under Article 151 of the Constitution, to be acted upon by the procedure laid down in that article?" (emphasis added).[19] Over 90 percent voted yes. Given that there are examples on both side of the argument, a statistical analysis may reveal patterns that allow us to draw firmer conclusions.

Experts in "informal logic" and rhetoric have generally concluded that there is "no general method of determining bias in arguments" (Walton 1991: 1). However, a statistical analysis may reveal a different answer. All caveats notwithstanding, using ordinary least squares and logistic regression analysis, it is possible to test which factors influence the outcome of referendums. Of course, such analyses can reveal only a statistical pattern, and it is important to be aware of the limitations of this method. Still, a statistical analysis can point in a general direction and give us a rough indication, which can be used to develop more qualitative explanations.

Using a sample of all the referendums on ethnic and national issues (referendums on independence or self-determination) since 1980 (based on Laponce 2010), and using the questions provided by the Centre for

Table 17. Emotive Words and Determinants of Referendum Outcomes in Polls on Independence or Home Rule

Variable	Model I	Model II	Model III	Model IV
Constant	29.8*	−1.76	51.7	81.1*
	(11.5)	(1.23)	(15.23)	(12.9)
Word count				−0.64*
				(0.307)
Emotive word	2.51	−0.491*	10.143	−16.9
	(2.18)	(1.05)	(13.123)	(11.8)
Political rights	5.86*			
	(2.18)			
N	21	74	21	21
r^2	.43	.42	.05	.30

Note:
*Statistically significant at .05

Research on Direct Democracy, a referendum question was classed as biased if it included the phrases "do you agree" or "do you approve" and was given the value of 1 if one of these words appeared. The referendum was given the value 0 if none of the words were included in the question.[20]

As the figures in Table 17 show, the presence of these words was not statistically significantly positive in any of the models. In fact, in Model II there was a slight tendency for emotive words to have a negative effect on the outcome of a referendum. However, if we exclude countries without a democratic system (here defined as having a score above 2 on the Freedom House Index), this effect disappears. It is difficult to conclude that the wording makes much of a difference.

Another possibility could be that voters tend to vote no if they are confused. Some of the earliest research into voting intentions in referendums found that "the elector, when in doubt, votes 'no' more often than 'yes'" (Schumacher 1932: 1), and more recent research has corroborated this finding (Bowler and Donovan 1998: 44). Based on this research, it could be speculated that a longer and more cumbersome question would be more likely to confuse voters. This hypothesis was tested by correlating the number of words in the ballot question with a yes vote on the referendum. There is some statistical evidence to suggest that longer questions are more likely to lead to a no vote, though the coefficient is less than one

(−0.64). The presence of a long question does not automatically lead to rejection of a proposed policy, but it is likely to marginally contribute to a higher percentage of no votes on referendums.

Conclusion

One of the objections to loaded questions is that the presence of words like "agree" or "approve" might create a bias and prompt the voters to vote for a proposition that they do not agree with. There have been several examples of referendums with "loaded" or "biased" questions, for example in East Timor, Québec, and Spain. Some of these referendums have been successful (e.g., in the devolution referendums in Spain); others have been unsuccessful (e.g., the referendum on sovereignty association in the Québec and autonomy for East Timor). As a general rule, biased questions have not altered the outcome of referendums, and the presence of words like "agree" or "approve" does *not* have a statistically significant impact on the outcome. If anything there is a slight tendency for the presence of one of these biased words to slightly decrease the yes vote and favor the opponents.

However, there is some evidence that longer questions on the ballot result in a higher no vote. One might speculate that this is due to confusion caused by longer, and hence less intelligible, questions. But the effect is small (−0.64), though it is statistically significant.

To summarize, when analyzing referendums on devolution and self-government held between 1980 and 2011, there is no evidence that biased words lure voters to support propositions that they disagree with. "The people is never corrupted, but it is often misled," wrote Jean-Jacques Rousseau in the *Social Contract* (Rousseau 1993: 765). Whatever the general philosophical truth of this statement, his conclusion is not supported if we focus on referendums on devolution and national self-determination. People are not "misled" by biased questions in referendums on devolution and independence issues.

Patterns and Tendencies in Ethnonational Referendums

"If you are in democratic politics you have to take account of what people are thinking and you have to keep listening to the people. Parties which don't do that fail badly." Tony Blair was characteristically confident and bold when he told the BBC why he submitted issues to referendums (April 20, 2004). Whether it was the idealistic concern for "what people are thinking" that motivated him, or whether it was the fear that he might "fail badly" had he not held referendums is an open question. The analyses carried out in this book mostly suggest that politicians are motivated by the latter. Generally speaking, referendums on ethnic and national issues have been held for strategic and *not* for idealistic reasons. But before looking at the conclusions, it is useful, once again, to go back to the starting point and restate the context within which these referendums have taken place. As I argued in this book, macro-political regulation of ethnic conflicts takes many forms, ranging from genocide at one extreme to democratically approved power sharing at the other end (McGarry and O'Leary 1994). Generally speaking we can distinguish three strategies. In the words of Arend Lijphart: "There are three types of solutions to deal with the political problems of a plural society. . . . One is to eliminate or substantially reduce the plural character of the society through assimilation. . . . The second is the consociational solution which accepts the plural divisions. . . . Especially if the second solution should be very unlikely to succeed or if it has been tried and failed, the remaining logical alternative is to reduce the pluralism by dividing the state into two or more separate and homogeneous states" (Lijphart 1977: 44). Each of these strategies can be endorsed—or rejected—by referendums, as they have been in celebrated examples like the Norwegian independence referendum in 1905 and in the nightmare scenarios of the former Yugoslavia in the early 1990s.

In addition to these policies—and accompanying referendums—we can add yet two other categories: right-sizing referendums and referendums on European integration. The former concern the tweaking of borders, typically referendums on whether a particular ethnic group, say the Germans in present-day North Schleswig, should be allowed to join their kin group across the border in the Federal Republic of Germany; the latter concern votes on whether to join the European Union and on whether or not to endorse further integration.

In this book we have distinguished five kinds of referendums:

- Difference-eliminating referendums
- Difference-managing referendums
- Right-sizing referendums
- Secession/partition referendums
- Referendums on European integration (somewhat outside the neat categorization)

The question we have explored in this book is when governments or others opt to hold these different referendums. When do governments choose to ask the people before opting for a policy with ethnic and national implications and consequences?

The overall tendency discerned in the book is—though with inevitable exceptions to the general rule—that ethnonational referendums often—but not always—conform with the competition proximity model, that is, the formal statement that says that the value of $(I_m - P_i)^2$ is small, then the probability of a referendum will be larger than 1. Formally speaking, referendums on ethnic and national issues (and European integration) are likely to be held if:

$$\sum_{i=1}^{n} \frac{C}{(I_m - P_i)^2} > 1,$$

where C is the competition the actor, i, is facing, and $(I_m - P_i)^2$ the squared distance between the actor's preference point P_i and the preference point of the median voter I_m.

Despite their differences, the referendums were generally motivated by strategic considerations. The statistical models and the accompanying case studies based on area specialists' and historians' accounts showed that ethnonational referendums, ceteris paribus, were held when (1) the initiator faced military, electoral, or political competition and (2) the initiator felt that he or she had a policy that chimed with a majority of the voters. From autocratic rulers like Napoleon in the nineteenth century to mild-mannered democrats like the Welsh first minister Rhodri Morgan in this century, the logic was the same. So strong is the evidence that this almost amounts to a universal law.

However, this was not the only general finding uncovered by statistical and historical studies. Based on an exhaustive list of more than the 200 ethnonational referendums held since 1791, we also found a distinct pattern to their use. In the book we tested—and found support for—the following hypotheses:

- Difference-eliminating referendums (defined as referendums on homogenizations/assimilation of different groups) tend to occur in undemocratic societies (defined as societies with Freedom House scores greater than 4).
- Difference-managing referendums tend to occur in countries with Freedom House scores at the most democratic end of the 7-point spectrum, and tend to occur following negotiated settlements to longstanding ethnic disagreements.
- Secession/partition referendums tend to occur following the lifting of a long-standing international hegemony—but only if there is a broadbased elite commitment to polyarchic government in the country in question (as was the case in the former Soviet republics of Estonia, Latvia, and Lithuania).
- Right-sizing referendums similarly tend to be held after profound changes in the international system (such as after World War I). Yet, according to our hypothesis, they are not held in the wake of wars. Countries—or armies—that are successful on the battlefield do not—according to our hypothesis—like to see their handiwork undone at the ballot box.

In addition to these hypotheses, we also found that ethnonational referendums do not result in exacerbations of conflict. We hypothesized that referendums lead to peaceful resolutions of conflicts only if two conditions are met: (1) there is elite consensus for the proposed solution and (2) international backing for (or not outright opposition to) the referendum. With certain exceptions, these hypotheses were corroborated. However, in the process of discerning these patterns we uncovered a number of other regularities. As we can see from the Table 18, the overwhelming number of the referendums fall in the category of secession referendums (82 of the 218 ethnonational referendums fall in this category—38 percent of the total). The second largest category (57 out of 218) is difference-managing referendums, which is only marginally ahead of right-sizing referendums (53 cases, or 24 percent). Difference-eliminating referendums are the rarest. Only 26 of 218 referendums were difference-eliminating referendums.

The vast majority of ethnonational referendums have taken place in Europe (including the former Soviet Union). These constitute fifty-six in total. While a relatively large number of referendums have taken place in Africa (twenty-two), half of these were the 1958 plebiscites instigated by President de Gaulle concerning the African colonies' continued membership in the Communauté française (eleven out of the twenty-two ethnonational referendums held in the continent) (Schmidt 2009). Perhaps surprising, given the presence of direct democracy at the local level there (Bowler and Donovan 1998), a very small number of ethnonational plebiscites have been held in North America. All seven referendums were held in Canada, with three of these involving attempts to settle the ethnic differences between Francophone and Anglophone Canadians (the referendums in Québec in 1980 and 1995 and the failed constitutional referendum over the Charlottetown Agreement in 1992). The other four referendums were in Nova Scotia in 1867, in Newfoundland in 1948, and in Nunavut in 1982 and 1998 (Légaré 1998). However, we must not forget that these referendums are not about commitment to mechanisms of direct democracy, but should be seen as a mechanism for legitimizing macro-ethnic policies. The lack of ethnonational referendums in North America is, consequently, not just a reflection of deeper seated values or commitments, but a consequence of deeper social and ethnic factors.

Given that Canada—at least at the time of writing—is the only North American country with an ethnically diverse population (something that might change if white Americans become a minority) (Roberts 2007: A1), it is perhaps not surprising that no ethnonational referendums have taken

Table 18. Ethnonational Referendums, 1791–2012

Country	Area	Year	Difference-eliminating	Difference-managing	Secession	Right-sizing
France	Avignon	1791				X
France	Savoy	1792				X
France	Nice	1792				X
Belgium	Wallonia	1793				X
France	Moselle	1793				X
France	Mulhouse	1798				X
France	Geneva	1798				X
France	Switzerland	1802			X	
Italy	Lombard	1848				X
Italy	Regio	1848				X
Russia	Moldova	1857				X
Italy	Parma	1860				X
Italy	Sicily	1860				X
Italy	Tuscany	1860				X
Italy	Naples	1860				X
Italy	Marches	1860				X
Italy	Ombrie	1860				X
France	Savoy	1860				X
United States	Texas	1861			X	
United States	Virginia	1861			X	
United States	Tennessee	1861			X	
Britain	Ionian Islands	1863				X
Italy	Venice	1866				X
Canada	Nova Scotia	1867		X		
Denmark	Virgin Islands	1868				X
Italy	Rome	1870				X
Sweden	Saint Barthélemy	1877				X
Australia	Tasmania	1898		X		
Australia	NSW	1898		X		
Australia	Victoria	1898		X		
Australia	South Australia	1898		X		
Australia	Western Australia	1898		X		
Australia	Queensland	1899		X		
Australia	South Australia	1899		X		
Australia	Tasmania	1899		X		
Australia	Victoria	1899		X		
Australia	New South Wales	1899		X		
Australia	Western Australia	1900		X		
Sweden	Norway	1905			X	
United Kingdom	Natal	1909				
Denmark	Iceland	1918		X		

Table 18. (continued)

Country	Area	Year	Difference-eliminating	Difference-managing	Secession	Right-sizing
Turkey	Kars, Batoumi	1918				X
Finland	Aaland	1919		X		
Austria	Vorarlberg	1919				X
Germany	North Schleswig	1920				X
Germany	South Schleswig	1920				X
Germany	Allenstein	1920				X
Belgium	Eupen	1920				X
Germany	Marienwerder	1920				X
Austria	Klagenfurt	1920				X
Germany	Upper Silesia	1921				X
Austria	Tyrol	1921				X
Austria	Salzburg	1921				X
Austria	Sophron	1921				X
United Kingdom	Rhodesia	1922		X		
Australia	Western Australia	1933			X	
Germany	Germany	1933	X			
Germany	Germany	1934	X			
Germany/France	Saar	1935				X
United States	Philippines	1935			X	
Germany	Germany	1936	X			
Germany/Austria	Germany/Austria	1938	X			
Denmark	Iceland	1944			X	
China	Mongolia	1945			X	
France	Brigant	1945				X
Poland	Poland	1946				X
South Africa	Namibia	1946	X			
Denmark	Faroe Islands	1946			X	X
India/Pakistan	Border	1947				X
Italy/France	Brigue	1947				X
United Kingdom	Newfoundland	1948				X
India	Jungadagh	1948				X
France	Chandernagor	1949				X
Belgium	Belgium	1950	X			
United States	Puerto Rico	1951		X		
India	Nagaland	1951			X	
United States	Virgin Islands	1954		X		
International	Saar	1955				X
France	Cambodia	1955			X	
United Kingdom	Malta	1956			X	
Ghana	Togoland	1956				X
France	Togo	1956			X	

Table 18. (continued)

Country	Area	Year	Difference-eliminating	Difference-managing	Secession	Right-sizing
Egypt/Syria	Egypt/Syria	1958	X			
France	French Somalia	1958			X	
France	New Caledonia	1958		X		
France	Saint Pierre and Miquelon	1958			X	
France	Polynesia	1958		X		
France	Guinea	1958			X	
France	Oubangui	1958			X	
France	Niger	1958			X	
France	Chad	1958			X	
France	Congo	1958			X	
France	Upper Volta	1958			X	
France	Dahomey	1958			X	
France	Soudan	1958			X	
France	Gabon	1958			X	
France	Senegal	1958			X	
France	Ivory Coast	1958			X	
France	Madagascar	1958			X	
France	Algeria	1958			X	
France	Mauritania	1958			X	
Egypt/Syria/Libya	Egypt/Syria/Libya	1958	X			
France/Algeria	France/Algeria	1961		X		
New Zealand	Western Samoa	1961			X	X
Cameroon		1961				X
West Indian Federation	Jamaica	1961			X	
Algeria/France	Algeria/France	1962			X	
Malaysia	Singapore	1962				X
Congo-Brazzaville	Congo-Brazzaville	1963	X			
France	Equatorial Guinea	1963			X	
Ghana	Ghana	1964	X			
United Kingdom	Malta	1964			X	
Benin	Benin	1964				
United Kingdom	Rhodesia	1964			X	
Somalia	Somalia	1967				X
France	Afars and Issas	1967				X
United States	Puerto Rico	1967		X		
Benin	Benin	1968	X			
Cameroon	Cameroon	1972	X			
Madagascar	Madagascar	1972	X			
United Kingdom	Northern Ireland	1973		X		

Table 18. (continued)

Country	Area	Year	Difference-eliminating	Difference-managing	Secession	Right-sizing
Congo B	Congo B	1973	X			
Guinea B	Guinea B	1973	X			
France	Comoros	1974			X	
New Zealand	Niue	1974			X	
France	Comores	1974			X	
India	Sikkim	1975				X
France	Mariannes	1975	X			
France	Mayotte	1976		X		
France	St. Pierre	1976		X		
South Africa	Southwest Africa	1977			X	
Philippines	Philippines	1977		X		
Netherlands	Aruba	1977			X	
France	Somalia	1977			X	
Ghana	Ghana	1978	X			
Sierra Leone	Sierra Leone	1978	X			
Micronesia	Micronesia	1978		X		
Denmark	Greenland	1979		X		
United Kingdom	Scotland	1979		X		
United Kingdom	Wales	1979		X		
Togo	Togo	1979	X			
United States	Virgin Islands	1979		X		
Congo B	Congo B	1979	X			
Spain	Basque Country	1979		X		
Spain	Catalonia	1979		X		
Canada	Northwest Territory	1979		X		
Canada	Québec	1980			X	
Spain	Andalusia	1980		X		
Spain	Galicia	1980		X		
United States	Guam	1982		X		
United States	Palau	1983		X		
North Cyprus	North Cyprus	1983	X			
United Kingdom	Cocos Islands	1984				X
Zaire	Zaire	1984	X			
Argentina	Beagle Channel	1984				X
Morocco	Morocco/Libya	1984	X			
Central African Republic	Central African Republic	1986	X			
Côte d'Ivoire	Côte d'Ivoire	1986	X			
Suriname	Suriname	1987		X		
Niger	Niger	1987	X			
France	New Caledonia	1987		X		

Table 18. (continued)

Country	Area	Year	Difference-eliminating	Difference-managing	Seces-sion	Right-sizing
Philippines	Philippines	1989		X		
Philippines	Philippines	1990		X		
Yugoslavia	Slovenia	1990			X	
United States	Palau	1990			X	
Burundi	Burundi	1991	X			
USSR	Lithuania	1991			X	
USSR	Estonia	1991			X	
USSR	Latvia	1991			X	
USSR	Georgia	1991			X	
USSR	Ukraine	1991			X	
USSR	USSR	1991	X			
USSR	Kourilles	1991				X
Georgia	South Ossetia	1991			X	
Georgia	Abkhazia	1991			X	
Yugoslavia	Croatia	1991			X	
Croatia	Serbs	1991			X	
Yugoslavia	Macedonia	1991			X	
USSR	Armenia	1991			X	
Bosnia	Serbs	1991			X	
Serbia	Sandjak	1991			X	
Serbia	Kosovo	1991			X	
USSR	Turkmenistan	1991			X	
USSR	Karabagh	1991			X	
USSR	Uzbekistan	1991			X	
Macedonia	Albanians	1991			X	
Moldova	Transnistie	1991			X	
Yugoslavia	Bosnia	1992			X	
Yugoslavia	Montenegro	1992			X	
Georgia	South Ossetia	1992			X	
Bosnia	Krajina	1992			X	
Canada	Canada	1992		X		
Ethiopia	Eritrea	1993			X	
Bosnia	Serbs	1993			X	
United States	Puerto Rico	1993		X		
Netherlands	Curacao	1993		X		
Georgia	Abkhazia	1995			X	
Québec	Cris	1995			X	
Canada	Québec	1995			X	
United Kingdom	Scotland	1997		X		
United Kingdom	Wales	1997		X		
Canada	Nunavut	1998		X		

Table 18. (continued)

Country	Area	Year	Difference-eliminating	Difference-managing	Seces-sion	Right-sizing
United Kingdom	Northern Ireland	1998		X		
Comoros	Anjouran	1998			X	
Sudan	Sudan	1998	X			
St. Kitts and Nevis		1998			X	
United States	Puerto Rico	1998		X		
Indonesia	East Timor	1999			X	
Somalia	Somaliland	2001			X	
France	Corsica	2003		X		
Cyprus	Cyprus	2004		X		
Burundi	Burundi	2005		X		
Spain	Catalonia	2006		X		
New Zealand	Tokelau	2006		X		
Yugoslavia	Montenegro	2006			X	
Algeria	Algeria	2007		X		
Spain	Andalusia	2007			X	
Denmark	Greenland	2008		X		
France	Mayotte	2009		X		
United Kingdom	Wales	2011		X		
Sudan	Southern Sudan	2011			X	
United States	Puerto Rico	2012		X		
Total			26	57	82	53

Source: Based on Laponce (2010); Centre for Research on Direct Democracy; Butler and Ranney (1978). Research assistance by Nina Bamford is greatly appreciated.

place in the United States. The same also explains why only a few ethnonational referendums have been held in Latin America, such as the referendum in Guatemala in 1999 (Chapman 2011).[1]

Another pattern worth noting is the historical spread of the referendums. There have been three peaks in the use of referendums: in the aftermath of World War I, during the period of decolonization, and following the breakup of the Soviet Union and the fall of communism. As we can see from the table there are distinct patterns. In the aftermath of World War I, there was a predominance of, respectively, difference-eliminating referendums and secession referendums. Most of these—with the exception of the Icelandic secession referendum—were organized in response to Woodrow Wilson's demand for national self-determination (Wambaugh 1933).

But in the other periods we see distinct patterns. In the period between 1945 and 1965 (the period during which most colonies gained their independence) we find a large number of difference-eliminating referendums (a total of nineteen) and a surprisingly smaller number of secession referendums (only six). In the period from 1976 to 1995, coinciding with the fall of authoritarian regimes in the Soviet Union (and in Western European countries like Spain, Portugal, and Greece), we see a growth in the number secession referendums. Most of these twenty-three secession referendums were plebiscites on independence in ten of the fourteen former member states of the Soviet Union and referendums in *all* of the former Yugoslav states except Serbia and the referendum in Kosovo in 1991. During this period, difference-eliminating referendums almost completely dried up, numbering only three—the most auspicious one being the 1992 referendum on maintaining the Soviet Union (Brady and Kaplan 1994).

The question is what accounts for these differences. The general pattern is that difference-eliminating referendums generally are held in polities where the level of political freedom/competition is low. Using Freedom House scores, we found that difference-eliminating referendums almost exclusively occur in countries with Freedom House scores above 4, such as Egypt, Libya, and Syria under Nasser and the African states before multiparty systems were established.

The remaining referendums support this pattern; to take but a few examples, the plebiscites to approve the merger of Singapore and Malaysia in 1962, and the referendum to preserve the Soviet Union in 1991 were held in countries that were not democratic. The conclusion is that difference-eliminating referendums, ceteris paribus, are held in polities that cannot be described as polyarchies. Not all referendums conform to a simple model. But it seems that most authoritarian regimes—no matter how undemocratic they are—subscribe to a version of the theory of "legitimacy by acclamation" espoused by the controversial German political theorist Carl Schmitt, who in the 1930s developed a case for the view that even autocratic rulers need to acquire support from their subjects, and that referendums are the most efficient and appropriate means of gaining this, as they do not involve political parties or representatives who may be seen as diluting the "pure" acclamation of the people.

Needless to say, such referendums are not always "free and fair," but in a surprising number of cases the voters have more or less freely accepted and endorsed autocratic rulers such as in Nazi Germany or in Egypt and Syria in the 1950s (Schmitt 1926).

This—many believe—is a strong case against any kind of direct democracy (Mac Ginty 2003). Anyone looking solely at the difference-eliminating plebiscites would agree that he had a point. But the same charge cannot be made against difference-managing referendums. These are almost exclusively held in polyarchies. The only exceptions are the Philippines, Suriname, and Burundi, which account for a small fraction of the cases. As outlined in detail in Chapter 2, this pattern is hardly surprising as difference management is part and parcel of democratic government. Multiethnic democracies are *polities* that already have accepted the need for policy accommodation. This was clearly the case in the 1998 referendum on the Good Friday Agreement in Northern Ireland, and in the referendums in Galicia, the Basque Country, and Catalonia in the beginning of the 1980s. It was also the case in the devolution referendums in Scotland and Wales in Britain, in Greenland in Denmark in 1980, and in the (albeit unsuccessful) Charlottetown referendum in Canada in 1992. However, this does not mean that these polls were held for idealistic reasons. In fact, as we saw, the difference-managing referendums too were largely held for strategic reasons and generally conform to the competition proximity model. It is less obvious that there is a pattern when it comes to the secession referendums. Secessions (and partitions, which cannot always been treated as similar—see the Schleswig case study in Chapter 4) take place under many conditions. Yet, one thing seems to characterize these polls; they take place after large changes in the tectonic plates of the international systems. The fall of communism is a case in point. Communism was able to put an autocratic lid on nationalist aspirations, as were colonial powers, of course, but unlike with the fall of communism, the dismantling of colonial empires did not open the floodgates of secessionist referendums. Referendums on secession—as we saw in the case study of the Soviet independence referendums in 1991—took place at a time where there was a stated (if often elite-based) demand for democracy. Thus in the former Soviet republics there was an aspiration for a more polyarchic system of government—something that was also present in the case of East Timor in 1999—and even in the case of Eritrea (although that ambition was soon thwarted by the government of Isaias Afewerki and the not so aptly named People's Front for Democracy and Justice) (Markakis 1995). These referendums were a consequence of this change toward democracy. As a corollary, the elites became aware that they needed to propose policies that strengthened their legitimacy. Holding referendums on popular issues was often a good way of doing this. Thus the competition proximity model explains secessionist referendums. We also found that right-sizing referendums (polls on where borders should be drawn) generally tended to corroborate the competition proximity model. And we found in Chapter 7 that referendums on European integration tend to follow the same logic. Thus this model generally tended to confirm the hypothesis that the EU is an issue that touches emotive heart strings and that politicians are willing to submit EU issues to a vote if this can strengthen their own domestic position, even if at the expense of "an ever closer union."

Violence and Ethnonational Referendums

As we saw in Chapters 3 and 5, referendums sometimes resolve conflicts peacefully (Schleswig being a case in point). Yet at other times plebiscites have led to exacerbation of conflicts—as was the case in the East Timor referendum, where "approximately 1000 people were killed and 200.000 were displaced in violence against the civil population after the referendum in 1999" (Bertrand 2004: 156). These dire consequences are perhaps among the reasons why some scholars are skeptical of referendums to resolve ethnic conflicts peacefully. Vernon Bogdanor, otherwise an enthusiast for direct democracy, bluntly stated in a book chapter on the subject that "referendums cannot be used for this" (Bogdanor 1996: 5). While such a sweeping statement is not warranted, referendums occasionally have resulted in bloodshed and violence, and not just difference-eliminating referendums (that almost goes without saying as these are held under undemocratic circumstances) but also other referendums. But generally, violence in the aftermath of a referendum is a rarity. While it is true that violence rarely accompanies difference-managing referendums, we are still in need of an explanation of why and when violence occurs. This is especially relevant regarding secession referendums.

As we saw in Chapter 4, it has become almost a universal norm that secessions and partitions require ratifications by the people in referendums, as was clearly shown in the cases of East Timor in 2001, Montenegro in 2006, and Southern Sudan in 2011. But when do such polls lead to violence?

And when (if at all) can they avoid bloodshed? It might be instructive to examine a couple of examples that we have considered in the previous chapters. In 1905 Norway seceded peacefully from Sweden, and many years later Eritrea did the same when splitting amicably from Ethiopia. These cases have little in common, except that they were peaceful. Conversely, in the aftermath of the referendum in East Timor in 1999, hostilities broke out that displaced 103,000 people and killed an estimated 14,000 people. Why? Both domestic and foreign politics played a role. Shortly after the death of President el-Hajj Mohammed Suharto, his successor, President Bacharuddin Jusuf Habibie, was pressured from many sides, not least the international community. When he took office, Habibie made it clear that independence for East Timor was out of the question, but that he would consider giving East Timor special autonomy. In January 1999, however, Habibie surprised everyone by announcing a plebiscite, saying that if the voters in East Timor did not vote for autonomy it would be seen as a vote for independence (Chopra 2002). This particular decision made Habibie extremely unpopular within Indonesia (Miller 2004). As a result of the opposition to the decision, there was no agreement on the ground rules, the administration of the poll, or practical issues—let alone an agreement on the legitimacy of employing the plebiscite to resolve the issue. Further- more, the United Nations Electoral Administration Unit, which normally gets involved in such referendums, did *not* administer the poll. The local UN mission (with some minimal assistance from the Australian Electoral Commission) organized the vote. However, the poll took place under con- stant threat from the Indonesian army. The result was that an emphatic vote against Jakarta was overshadowed by violence.

A similar outcome resulted in 1992 when the Bosnians voted for se- cession from Yugoslavia. The European Communities (they were yet to become the European Union) gave—through the much criticized Badinter Commission (Radan 2000: 47)—the thumps up for the vote and arguably failed to recognize that democracy is more than just majority voting. The outcome of the vote was clear and unequivocal. A total of 92 percent said yes to independence, on a 64 percent turnout. The Serbs in the province responded by organizing a poll of their own in the enclave where there was a Serbian majority. Predictably (and under conditions that were a far cry from those outlined in Chapter 8), 92 percent of the voters voted to remain in Yugoslavia. The referendum resulted in antagonized and entrenched positions. The struggle continued in Clausewitz-like fashion, by "other means," that is, through war. Based on these examples, it is not surprising that referendums on ethnonational issues have gotten a bad name. But is the name fair? Not entirely, especially as other referendums (such as the aforementioned polls in Norway, Schleswig, Eritrea, and Montenegro) have resulted in peaceful solutions! What were the reasons that the latter examples resulted in peace, whereas the cases of Bosnia-Herzegovina and East Timor resulted in war? Based on the analyses we found that there are two factors involved in nonviolent referendums: (1) the international community guarantees proper conduct of the referendum and recognizes the result and (2) the referendum is the result of a negotiation between both sides. As we saw in Chapter 6, no referendum is worth the ballot paper it is printed on if the international community does not recognize the new state. When Turkey was the only country in the world that recognized Northern Cyprus after the referendum in 1975, it did not resolve the conflict but merely led to further tension with the Greek-speaking south. Similarly, when South Ossetia voted for independence in 2002, the result merely caused further tensions between Russia and Georgia.

But when does the international community accept the outcome of an ethnonational referendum. All other things being equal (and this qualification and other caveats are necessary), referendum results are accepted by the international community when these conditions are met: the new state (or the new internal organization of a state) is not threatening to its neighbors and the referendum follows international standards (see Chapter 4). In addition to these conditions, another (and perhaps more important) condition is that the parties themselves agree to a referendum (as in the case of the referendum in Southern Sudan in January 2011). However, it should be noted that the "peace" in Southern Sudan is a fragile one, and nothing is certain at this time.

As a general rule referendums result in peaceful outcomes *only* when *both parties* agree on the legitimacy of a referendum. This was the case in Northern Ireland in 1998. The difference-managing referendum was a result of a negotiation among all the major parties, whereas the difference-eliminating referendum in 1973 was one-sided.

The same logic was present in the case of Montenegro (Tierney 2012: 173). The difference-managing referendum in 1993 was a result of a bilateral negotiation, as was the secession/partition referendum in 2006. In the latter case the Serbian and Montenegrin governments agreed (with EU as intermediaries) to a political divorce settlement. This need for an agreement is why legal issues are important. As we saw in Chapter 4, the legal barriers to holding a referendum are often high. As a general rule, at least in the countries surveyed, there is no right to hold a referendum on secession, nor is there a right to do so in public international law.

To summarize, referendums, as a general rule, do not result in violence when the international community accepts the result and when the two parties agree to hold a referendum (and agree to the conduct of the poll). This—to take another example—is what happened in 1920 when the Danes and the Germans (with the backing of the international community) agreed that the conflict could be resolved through a referendum. The Danes and the Germans had fought two wars (1848–50 and 1864) over the Sønderjylland/ Schleswig territory. No solution seemed possible. This situation prompted Lord Palmerstone to quip, "Only three people . . . have ever really understood the Schleswig-Holstein business—the Prince Consort, who is dead—a German professor, who has gone mad—and I, who have forgotten all about it" (quoted in Kissinger 1994: 58). In the aftermath of World War I the conflict was solved, not through war or high diplomacy but through a referendum accepted by both parties—and after both sides had recognized the right of the other. This, perhaps, is not so much due to any inherent quality in the referendum, but recognition of the fact that, to quote John Stuart Mill: "One of the most indispensable requisites in the practical conduct of politics is conciliation: a readiness to compromise; a willingness to concede something to opponents and to shape good measures so as to be as little offensive as possible to persons of opposite views" (Mill 2008: 385). It is only when referendums are held in this spirit of compromise and conciliation that balloting can stop bullets.

Legislation and Litigation

Primary Legislation

Australia
    Commonwealth Electoral Act 1918
Canada
    Clarity Act 2000
    Québec 1978 Referendum Act
India
    India Independence Act of 18 July 1947
Montenegro
    Law on the State-Legal Status of the Republic of Montenegro 2005
New Zealand
    Citizen Initiated Referenda Act 1993
Scotland
    Mental Health (Public Safety and Appeals) (Scotland) Act 1999
Sudan
    Southern Sudan Referendum Act 2009
United Kingdom
    Act of Union 1707
    Constitutional Reform Act 2005
    Government of Wales Act 1998
    Mental Health (Public Safety and Appeals) (Scotland) Act 1999
    Northern Ireland Act 1998
    Political Parties, Elections and Referendum Act 2001
    Scotland Act 1998

Secondary Legislation

Australia
  New South Wales Local Government (Elections) Regulation 1998
United Kingdom
  Local Authorities (Conduct of Referendums) (Wales) Regulations 2004

Litigation

Australia
  Wilson v. Independent Broadcasting Authority, SLT 279 (1979)
Canada
  Reference re: Secession of Quebec, 161 DLR (4th) 385 (1998)
European Court of Human Rights
  Matthews v. United Kingdom, 28 EHRR 361 (1999)
International Court of Justice
  Portugal v. Australia, ICJ Report 90–106 (June 30, 1995)
  Advisory Opinion on Western Sahara, ICJ Report 12–68, 55 (October 16, 1975)
Ireland
  Crotty v. An Taoiseach, IESC 4 (1987)
  McKenna v. An Taoiseach and Others, Defendants (No. 2), S.C. (1995)
United Kingdom
  Anderson, Reid and Doherty v. Scottish Ministers, UKPC D5 HRLR 6 (2001)
  R (Countryside Alliance) v. A-G, UKHL 56, [2006] 1 AC 262
Scotland
  Imperial Tobacco Ltd. v. Lord Advocate, CSIH 9 (2012)
UK Supreme Court and House of Lords
  AXA General Insurance Ltd. v. The Lord Advocate, 3 WLR 871 (2011)
  Madzimbamutu v. Lardner-Burke, 1 AC 64 (1969)
  Martin and Miller v. HM Advocate, UKSC 10 (2010)
  Pepper (Inspector of Taxes) v. Hart, AC 593 (1993)
  R (Jackson and Other) v. Attorney General, UKHL 56 (2005)
  Robinson v. Secretary of State for Northern Ireland, UKHL 32 (2002)
United States
  Kohlhaas v. Alaska, 147 P 3d 714 (2006).
  Texas v. White, 74 U.S. 700 (1868).

Notes

Introduction

1. In ancient Athens a "deme" was a subdivision of Attica. Demes, as simple subdivisions of land, seem to have existed in the sixth century B.C. and earlier, but did not acquire political significance until the reforms of Cheisthenes in 508 B.C., when enrollment in a deme became a requirement for citizenship and hence voting rights (Hansen 1999: 46).

2. "Scottish Independence: 'Corby Should Have Vote,'" *BBC News*, October 29, 2012, http://www.bbc.co.uk/news/uk-england-northamptonshire-20122435 (accessed December 11, 2012).

3. In the literature some have suggested that referendums differ from plebiscites, as the latter are polls held by authoritarian rulers to gain legitimacy for their policies. This distinction is common in French; see Denquin (1976).

4. For a good example, see Munro (1928). For a more recent example, see Grofman (2007).

5. On this subject, see De Dijn (1986) and Talaska (1988).

6. Milton Friedman (1966: 5). Perhaps it should also be added that the realism of these assumptions is of minor importance. As Friedman noted, "Truly important and significant hypotheses will be found to have 'assumptions' that are wildly inaccurate descriptive representations of reality, and, in general, the more significant the theory, the more unrealistic the assumptions (in this sense). The reason is simple. A hypothesis is important if it 'explains' much by little, that is, if it abstracts the common and crucial elements from the mass of complex and detailed circumstances surrounding the phenomena to be explained and permits valid predictions on the basis of them alone" (Friedman 1966: 12).

7. This methodology has of course been criticized by several, including Imre Lakatos, Thomas Kuhn, and Paul Feyerabend. See further Magee (2001: 221).

8. See Duverger (1972: 23–32).

9. Freedom House Scores are a statistical index developed by the U.S.-based Freedom House. For methodology see: www.freedomhouse.org.

10. I have dealt with this at some length in Qvortrup (2003: chap. 5).

Chapter 1. The History and Logic of Ethnonational Referendums, 1791–1945

1. Bajer (1914: 25): "Jeg kan ikke engang samtykke i at tage det ad referendum. Mine Instruktioner forbyder mig at samtykke" (I cannot even consent to submit the matter ad referendum. My instructions forbid me to consent) (translation by the author).

2. Colonial parliaments failed to approve the first draft of the constitution, and the decision to hold a referendum was reached only after the members of a constitutional convention were elected. See Stuart MacIntyre (2004: 136).

3. See Australian Electoral Commission (2011).

Chapter 2. Difference-Managing Referendums

1. See Rocard (1988).

2. See http://www.electionguide.org/country-news.php?ID = 248 (accessed July 30, 2012).

3. The fallacy of *post hoc ergo propter hoc* can arguably be traced back to Zeno of Elea (Gottlieb 2000: 67).

Chapter 3. Secession and Partition

1. Between 1918 and 1962, Yemen was a monarchy ruled by the Hamidaddin family. In 1962, North Yemen became a republic, but the United Kingdom maintained a protective area around the South Arabia port of Aden, which it had created in the nineteenth century. Britain withdrew in 1967 and the area became South Yemen. In 1970, the southern government adopted a Marxist-Leninist government. The two countries were formally united as the Republic of Yemen in 1990. See Burrowes (1991).

2. Stephen Tierney, http://www.ejiltalk.org/sudan%E2%80%99s-lesson-for-secession-a-comment/, Accessed September 1, 2011.

3. By contrast, "countries" like South Ossetia, Somaliland, and Northern Cyprus were not former colonies or dependent territories, hence they were not granted international recognition—despite the fact that they held referendums that were not unfair by international standards. See Initiative & Referendum Institute (2001).

4. I owe thanks to Professor Markku Suksi for this information.

5. The author was a member of a negotiation team under the U.S. State Department in Sudan in 2009.

6. Out of the 581 votes cast in the referendum on February 11, 2006, 349 (or 61 percent) were in favor of independence.

7. It is possible that the issue will be voted on again in the future. The leader of the largest group of overseas Tokelauans (the Tokelauan community in the Hutt Valley in New Zealand), Henry Joseph, called for another vote within two years, with the required approval being changed to a simple majority. See http://www.scoop.co.nz/stories/HL0710/S00392.htm.

Chapter 4. Ethnonational Referendums in Constitutional Law

1. For example, in *Anderson, Reid and Doherty v. Scottish Ministers* (2001) patients unsuccessfully challenged the Mental Health (Public Safety and Appeals) (Scotland) Act 1999.

2. This view has been taken by Dr. Aileen McHarg and Professor Tom Mullen. See Dinwoodie (2012).

Chapter 5. Right-Sizing Referendums

1. The word "irredentism"—as the etymology suggests—grew from Il Risorgimento. The word was used as part the concept of *Italia irredenta* ("unredeemed Italy"). This originally referred to Austro-Hungarian rule over mostly or partly Italian-inhabited territories such as Trentino, Trieste, Istria, and Dalmatia during the nineteenth and early twentieth centuries (Wirth 1936).

2. Some of the methodological issues are discussed in Campos and Kuzeyev (2007).

3. The referendum was acknowledged by Article 3 of the India Independence Act of July 18, 1947.

4. According to the Resolution of the Commission of January 5, 1949, "The question of the accession of the State of Jammu and Kashmir to India or Pakistan will be decided through the democratic method of a free and impartial plebiscite."

Chapter 6. Difference-Eliminating Referendums

1. Carl Schmitt was a controversial figure due to his role as legal adviser to the Nazi regime. The Kronjurist for the Nazi regime wrote apologies for the Führer and expressed views on Jews and other minorities that are anything but palatable; see, e.g., Schmitt (1934). Carl Schmitt was a Nazi and went to great lengths to defend the regime's anti-Semitism (Schmitt 1936).

2. In fact, de Gaulle made this remark in a conversation with Govenor-General Félix Adolphe Éboué of Chad on the eve of the referendums on whether the former colonies wanted to become members of the French Community (Communauté française) in 1958.

3. On Gorbachev more generally, see Brown (1996).

4. Model II is an ordinary least squares regression, which consequently does not have a Wald score, as this is a feature only of logistic regression models.

5. The Freedom House score is a negative measure. The higher the score (maximum of 7), the less democratic the country.

Chapter 8. Regulation of Ethnonational Referendums

1. Those interested in a more legalistic analysis should consult Vienna Commission (2002).

2. Despite an agreement reached in 1988, which stipulated that the electorate should include all Western Saharans counted in the 1974 census undertaken by the Spanish authorities, no vote has taken place (Jensen 2005: 137).

3. See http://www.un.org/peace/etimor99/agreement/agreeFrame_Eng03.html.

4. See http://www.un.org/peace/etimor99/agreement/agreeFrame_Eng03.html.

5. See United Nations (1993).

6. See Council of Europe (2001).

7. The author was a member of a group of experts sent out to mediate by U.S. President Barack Obama's Special Envoy General Scott Gration in 2009.

8. In other countries the Referendum Commissions are a subsection of the electoral commission. For example, in Australia the Electoral Commission is a permanent body. The same is true in the United Kingdom. The Australian Commission was established under the Commonwealth Electoral Act 1918; the U.K. Electoral Commission was established in 2001 under the Political Parties Elections and Referendum Act 2001.

9. The 1983 Constitution of St Kitts and Nevis states, "38.—(2) b) [a constitutional amendment must be] approved on a referendum by not less than two-thirds of all the votes validity cast on that referendum in the island of Saint Christopher and two-thirds of all the votes validly cast on that referendum in the island of Nevis."

10. An *abrogative referendum* is a plebiscite on an already existing law initiated by the voters.

11. A decision-making referendum is a referendum initiated by elected representatives.

12. The relevant sections of legislation are as follows: Azerbaijan (Article 139.1 of the election code); Bulgaria (electoral legislation); Croatia (Article 87.4); Italy (legislative regulation, abrogative referendum); Latvia (Article 79; it applies to constitutional revision); Malta (Article 20.1 of the Referenda Act); Portugal (Article 115.11); Poland (binding if 50 percent of electors participate—Article 125.3; 50 percent majority—no threshold—required for constitutional reform—Article 235.6); Russian Federation (electoral legislation); Slovakia (Article 98.1); Slovenia (Article 170.2); and the Former Yugoslav Republic of Macedonia (Article 73.2). See Council of Europe (2005).

13. See www.electoralcommission.org.uk/_.../Purdah_18887-13975_E_N_S_W_ .pdf (accessed January 10, 2010).

14. Elizabeth Gerber has found that campaign spending in support of a proposition was ineffectual. However, negative campaign spending, that is, spending against a proposition, was often effective (Gerber 1999).

15. In a 1998 amendment, contributions were limited to $3,000 per donor to each campaign (Québec 1978 Referendum Act). The 1998 amendment states, "The total of contributions to each national committee by the same elector in the same referendum shall not exceed the amount of $3,000" (Section 91).

16. See also the Local Authorities (Conduct of Referendums) (Wales) Regulations 2004.

17. House of Commons Research Reports 00/3, "Referendums: The New Rules."

18. See "The Funding of Political Parties in the United Kingdom" (Cm 4413, July 1999), chap. 9.

19. The question in Spanish was "¿Da usted su acuerdo a la ratificación de la iniciativa, prevista en el artículo 151 de la Constitución, a efectos de su tramitación por el procedimiento previsto en dicho artículo?"

20. The wording of the question is based on data provided by Centre for Research on Direct Democracy (www.c2d.ch).

Conclusion

1. In 1999, the Guatemalan population voted to approve or reject the constitutional reforms drafted as a way of implementing some of the most important agreements reached in the peace accords signed on December 29, 1996. Fewer than one in five registered voters turned out: 18.5 percent, or 757,978 of a total of 4,058,832 eligible voters (Chapman 2011).

Bibliography

Alapuro, R. (1988). *State and Revolution in Finland.* Berkeley: University of California Press.

Aldrich, J., J. Alt, and A. Lupia. (2010). "The EITM Approach: Origins and Interpretations." In J. Box-Steffensmeier, H. E. Brady, and D. Collier (eds.), *The Oxford Handbook of Political Science.* Oxford: Oxford University Press, 828–843.

Aldrich, R. (1993). *France in the South Pacific Since 1940.* London: Macmillan.

Altman, D. (2011). *Direct Democracy Worldwide.* Cambridge: Cambridge University Press.

Anderson, M. (1994). *Frontiers: Territory and State Formation.* Cambridge: Polity Press.

Aristotle. (1905). *The Politics of Aristotle.* J. E. C. Welldon (trans.). London: Macmillan.

Australian Electoral Commission (AEC). (2011). *Federation Fact Sheet 1—The Referendums 1898–1900.* http://www.aec.gov.au/About_AEC/Publications/Fact_Sheets/factsheet1.htm (accessed June 30, 2011).

Baimbridge, M. (2007). *The 1975 Referendum on Europe: Current Analysis and Lessons for the Future.* Vol. 2. London: Imprint Academic.

Bajer, F. (1914). *Da det danske Schleswig gik tabt.* Copenhagen: Rasmussen og Olsens Bogtrykkeri.

Bak, J. S. (1975). "Nationalliberale partipolitiske organisationer—Martsforeningen og Den Danske Folkeforenings opbygning og virke 1864–66." *Historisk Tidsskrift,* 75, 274–320.

Baran, H. (1998). "Democratic Theory of Political Self-Determination for a New World Order." In P. B. Lehning (ed.), *Theories of Secession.* London: Routledge, 32–59.

Basedau, M. (2011). "Parties in Chains: Do Ethnic Party Bans in Africa Promote Peace?" *Party Politics,* 17(1), 205–222.

Bateson, G. (1962). *Steps to an Ecology of Mind.* Chicago: University of Chicago Press.

Beigbeder, Y. (1994). *International Monitoring of Plebiscites, Referenda and National Elections: Self-Determination and Transition to Democracy.* Dordrecht: Martinus Nijhoff.

Bensa, A. (2003). *Nouvelle Calédonie: Un paradis en tourmente.* Paris: Découvertes Gallimard.

Bertrand, J. (2004). *Nationalism and Ethnic Conflict in Indonesia.* Cambridge: Cambridge University Press.

Bjørklund, T. (1982). "The Demand for Referendum: When Does It Arise and When Does It Succeed?" *Scandinavian Political Studies,* 5(2), 237–259.

———. (1996). "The Three Nordic 1994 Referenda Concerning Membership in the EU." *Cooperation and Conflict,* 31(1), 11–36.

———. (2003). *Om Folkeavstemninger: Norge og Norden 1905–1994.* Oslo: Universitetsforlaget.

Bogdanor, V. (1981a). *The People and the Party System: The Referendum and Electoral Reform in British Politics.* Cambridge: Cambridge University Press.

———. (1981b). "Referendums and Separatism II." In A. Ranney (ed.), *The Referendum Device.* Washington, D.C.: American Enterprise Institute, 143–160.

———. (1996). *Politics and the Constitution: Essays in British Government.* Dartmouth: Aldershot.

Bowler, S., and T. Donovan. (1998). *Demanding Choices: Opinion, Voting and Direct Democracy.* Ann Arbor: University of Michigan Press.

Brady, H. E., and C. S. Kaplan. (1994). "Eastern Europe and the Former Soviet Union." In D. Butler and A. Ranney (eds.), *Referendums Around the World: The Growing Use of Direct Democracy.* London: Macmillan, 174–217.

Bringa, T. R. (1993). "Nationality Categories, National Identification and Identity Formation in 'Multinational' Bosnia." *Anthropology of East Europe Review,* 11(1–2), 80–89.

Brown, A. (1996). *The Gorbachev Factor.* Oxford: Oxford University Press.

Buechi, R. (2012). "Use of Direct Democracy in the Jura Conflict." In W. Marxer (ed.), *Direct Democracy and Minorities.* Heidelberg: Springer Verlag, 181–194.

Burrowes, R. D. (1991). "Prelude to Unification: The Yemen Arab Republic, 1962–1990." *International Journal of Middle East Studies,* 23(4), 483–506.

Büthe, T. (1995). *European Union and National Electorates: The Austrian Public Debate and Referendum on Joining the European Union in June 1994.* Cambridge, Mass.: Harvard University, Minda de Gunzburg Center for European Studies.

Butler, D., and A. Ranney. (1978). "Practice." In D. Butler and A. Ranney (eds.), *Referendums: A Comparative Study of Practice and Theory.* Washington, D.C.: American Enterprise Institute for Public Policy Research, 3–22.

Campos, N. F., and V. S. Kuzeyev. (2007). "On the Dynamics of Ethnic Fractionalization." *American Journal of Political Science,* 51, 620–639.

Carr, E. H. (1942). *The Conditions of Peace.* New York: Macmillan.

Carrell, S. (2012). "Scottish Independence Panel Suggests Referendum Question, The Guardian, 22 August, A4."

Chapman, C. (2011). "Transitional Justice and the Rights of Minorities and Indigenous Peoples." In A. Paige (ed.), *Identities in Transition: Challenges for Transitional Justice in Divided Societies.* Cambridge: Cambridge University Press, 251–270.

Chopra, C. (2002). "Building State Failure in East Timor." *Development and Change*, 33, 979–1000.

Claude, I. (1955). *National Minorities: An International Problem*. Cambridge, Mass.: Harvard University Press.

Closa, C. (2007). "Why Convene Referendums? Explaining Choices in EU Constitutional Politics." *Journal of European Public Policy*, 14(8), 1311–1132.

Cohen, J. W. (1988). *Statistical Power Analysis for the Behavioural Sciences*. Hillsdale, N.J.: Lawrence Erlbaum.

Connor, W. (1994). *Ethnonationalism: The Quest for Understanding*. Princeton, N.J.: Princeton University Press.

Cordell, K., and S. Wolff. (2010). *Ethnic Conflict: Causes, Consequences and Responses*. Cambridge: Polity Press.

Cosgrove, R. A. (1981). *Albert Venn Dicey: Victorian Jurist*. London: Macmillan.

Council of Europe. (2001). "Interim Report on the Constitutional Situation of the Federal Republic of Yugoslavia" (CDL-INF(2001)023).

———. (2005). "Le référendum en Europe—Analyse des règles juridiques des Etats européens—Rapport adopté par le Conseil des élections démocratiques lors de sa 14e réunion (Venise, 20 octobre 2005) et la Commission de Venise lors de sa 64e session plénière (Venise, 21–22 octobre 2005)."

Cronin, T. (1989). *Direct Democracy: The Politics of Initiative, Referendum and Recall*. Cambridge, Mass.: Harvard University Press.

Davies, J. A. (1997). "Italy: 1796–1870: The Risorgimento." In George Holmes (ed.), *The Oxford Illustrated History of Italy*. Oxford: Oxford University Press, 177–209.

De Dijn, H. (1986). "Conceptions of Philosophical Method in Spinoza: Logica and mos geometricus." *Review of Metaphysics*, 40(1), 55–78.

Delaney, D., and H. Leitner. (1997). "The Political Construction of Scale." *Political Geography*, 16(2), 93–98.

Denquin, J.-M. (1976). *Référendum et plébiscite*. Paris: Librairie générale de droit et de jurisprudence.

De Winter, L., and P. Dumont. (1999). "Belgium: Party System(s) on the Eve of Disintegration?" In D. Broughton (Editor) *Changing Party Systems in Western Europe*. London: Pinter, 183–206.

Dicey, A. V. (1890). "Ought the Referendum to be Introduced into England?" *Contemporary Review*, 57, 486–512.

———. (1911). *A Leap in the Dark*. 2nd ed. London: John Murray.

———. (1981). *An Introduction to the Study of the Law of the Constitution*. Indianapolis: Liberty Fund.

Dinwoodie, R. (2012, February 11). "Holyrood Has Authority over the Referendum." *Herald*. http://www.heraldscotland.com/politics/political-news/holyrood-has-authority-over-referendum.1328929454 (accessed April 15, 2012).

Dür, A., and G. Mateo. (2011). "To Call or Not to Call? Political Parties and Referendums on the EU's Constitutional Treaty." *Comparative Political Studies*, 44(4), 468–492.

Duverger, M. (1972). "Factors in a Two-Party and Multiparty System." In M. Duverger (ed.), *Party Politics and Pressure Groups*. New York: Thomas Y. Crowell, 23–32.

Dworkin, R. (1982). "Law as Interpretation." *Texas Law Review*, 60, 527–551.

Eden, N. (1905). *Sweden for Peace*. Almqvist & Wiksell, Uppsala.

El Pais. (2005, January 5). "Periodistas, futbolistas y actors abren el viernes la campaña del referendum europeo."

Evans, J. A. (2002). "In Defence of Sartori Party System Change, Voter Preference Distributions and Other Competitive Incentives." *Party Politics*, 8(2), 155–174.

Evans, R. J. (2005). *The Third Reich in Power 1933–1939*. London: Allen Lane.

Farley, L. T. (1986). *Plebiscites and Sovereignty: The Crisis of Political Legitimacy*. Boulder, Colo.: Westview.

Fisch, W. B. (2006). "Constitutional Referendum in the United States of America." *American Journal of Comparative Law*, 54, 485–500.

Forman, J. C. (1975). *Den internationale Kommissions neutraliseringsforanstaltninger ved folkeafstemninger i Sønderjylland 1920*. Århus: Aarhus Universitetsforlag.

Franklin, M., M. Marsh, and L. McLaren. (1994). "Uncorking the Bottle: Popular Opposition to European Unification in the Wake of Maastricht." *Journal of Common Market Studies*, 32(4), 455–472.

Freudenthal, F. (1891). *Die Volksabstimmung bei Gebietsabtretungen und Eroberungen. Eine Studie aus dem Völkerrecht*. Erlangen: Th. Blaesing.

Friedman, M. (1966). "The Methodology of Positive Economics." In *Essays in Positive Economics*. Chicago: University of Chicago Press., 3–43.

Friis, K. (2007). "The Referendum in Montenegro: The EU's Postmodern Diplomacy." *European Foreign Affairs Review*, 12(1), 67–88.

Gallagher, M. (1996). "Conclusion." In M. Gallagher and P. Vincenzo Uleri (eds.), *The Referendum Experience in Europe*. Basingstoke: Macmillan, 226–252.

Gallup, G. (1941). "Question Wording in Public Opinion Polls." *Sociometry*, 4(3), 259–268.

Ganguly, S., and K. Bajpai. (1994). "India and the Crisis in Kashmir." *Asian Survey*, 34(5), 401–416.

Garrett, E. (2008). "Legislation and Statutory Interpretation." In K. Whittington, R.D. Keleman and G.A. Caldeira (editors) *The Oxford Handbook of Law and Politics*. Oxford: Oxford University Press, 360–377.

Geertz, C. (1973). "Thick Description: Toward an Interpretive Theory of Culture." In *The Interpretation of Cultures: Selected Essays*. New York: Basic Books, 3–30.

Gerber, E. (1999). *The Populist Paradox: Group Influence and the Promise of Direct Legislation*. Princeton, N.J.: Princeton University Press.

Gillies, D. (1998). "The Duhem Thesis and the Quine Thesis." In M. Curd and J. A. Cover (eds.), *Philosophy of Science: The Central Issues*. New York: Norton, 302–319.

Goodhart, P. (1971). *The Referendum*. London: Stacey.

Gottlieb, A. (2000). *The Dream of Reason*. London: Penguin.

Greenfield, L., and J. Eastwood. (2005). "Nationalism in Comparative Perspective." In T. Janoski (ed.), *Handbook of Political Sociology*. New York: Cambridge University Press, 33–53.

Grofman, B. (2007). "Toward a Science of Politics?" *European Political Science*, 6(2), 143–155.

Guibernau, M. (2000). "Spain: Catalonia and the Basque Country." *Parliamentary Affairs*, 53(1), 55–68.

Gunther, R., G. Sani, and G. Shabad. (1988). *Spain After Franco: The Making of a Competitive Party System*. Berkeley: University of California Press.

Habermas, J. (1996). "National Unification and Popular Sovereignty." *New Left Review*, 219, 3–13.

Hajnal, Z. L., E. R. Gerber, and H. Louch. (2002). "Minorities and Direct Legislation: Evidence from California Ballot Proposition Elections." *Journal of Politics*, 64(1), 154–177.

Hammerich, P. (1976). *Fred og nye farer*. Vol. 1. Copenhagen: Gyldendal.

Hannum, H. (2011). *Autonomy, Sovereignty, and Self-Determination: The Accommodation of Conflicting Rights*. Philadelphia: University of Pennsylvania Press.

Hansen, M. H. (1999). *The Athenian Democracy in the Age of Demosthenes: Structure, Principle and Ideology*. Norman: University of Oklahoma Press.

Harder, T. (2006). *Italien: Fra Mazzini til Berlusconi*. Copenhagen: Gyldendal.

Harmonia. (2010). "Knesset Approves Law Requiring Referendum for Land Withdrawals." *Harmonia*, 25, XIII, no. 635, 1.

Harrington, A. (2007). "Ethnicity, Violence and Land and Property Disputes in Timor-Leste." *East Timor Law Journal*, 2(1), 35–37.

Harris, E. (2002). *Nationalism and Democratisation: Politics of Slovakia and Slovenia*. Aldershot: Ashgate.

He, B. (2002). "Referenda as a Solution to the National-Identity/Boundary Question: An Empirical Assessment of the Theoretical Literature." *Alternatives*, 27(1), 67–97.

Hegel, G. W. F. (1832/1976). *Grundlinien der Philosophie des Rechts—Oder Naturrecht und Staatswissenschaft im Grundrisse. Mit Hegels eigenhändigen Motizen und mündlichen Zusätzen*. In O. Moldhauer and K. M. Michael (eds.), *Hegels Werke in Zwanzig Banden*. Frankfurt am Main: Suhrkamp Verlag, 434–532.

———. (1995) [1837]. *The Philosophy of History*. Indianapolis: Hacker.

Hegge, P. E. (2010). "Christian Michelsen: Slagkraft Ja—Dokumentlesning: Nei." In G. Forr, P. E. Hegge, and O. Njolstad (eds.), *Mellem Plikt og Lyst: Norske Statsministre 1873–2010*. Oslo: Dinamo Forlag, 197–210.

Hibbert, C. (1987). *Garibaldi and His Enemies*. New York: Penguin Books.

Hitler, A. (1934). *Reichsgesetzblatt*. Berlin: Kanzlerei.

———. (1972). *Mein Kampf*. Tiptree: Houghton Mifflin.

Hobolt, S. B. (2005). "When Europe Matters: The Impact of Political Information on Voting Behaviour in EU Referendums." *Journal of Elections, Public Opinion & Parties*, 15(1), 85–109.

———. (2006). "Direct Democracy and European Integration." *Journal of European Public Policy*, 13(1), 153–166.

———. (2009). *Europe in Question: Referendums on European Integration*. Oxford: Oxford University Press.

Hobsbawm, E. J., and D. J. Kertzer. (1992). "Ethnicity and Nationalism in Europe Today." *Anthropology Today*, 8(1), 3–8.

Hoffmann, E. (1992). "Folkeafstemninger og Demokrati." *Vandkunsten* 7, 59–70.

Horowitz, D. L. (1985). *Ethnic Groups in Conflict*. Berkeley: University of California Press.

Howells, C. A. (2006). *The Cambridge Companion to Margaret Atwood*. Cambridge: Cambridge University Press.

Hug, S. (2002). *Voices of Europe: Citizens, Referendums, and European Integration*. Lanham, Md.: Rowman & Littlefield.

Hug, S., and G. Tsebelis. (2002). "Veto Players and Referendums Around the World." *Journal of Theoretical Politics*, 14(4), 465–515.

Initiative & Referendum Institute. (2001). *Final Report of the Initiative & Referendum Institute's Election Monitoring Team*. Washington, D.C.: Citizen Lawmaker Press.

Innes, A. (2001). *Czechoslovakia: The Short Good Bye*. New Haven, Conn.: Yale University Press.

International Institute for Democracy and Electoral Assistance (IDEA). (2008). *Direct Democracy: The International IDEA Handbook*. Stockholm: IDEA.

Jansson, E. (1991). "The Frontier Province: Khudai Khidmatgars and the Muslim League." In D. A. Low (ed.), *The Political Inheritance of Pakistan*. London: Macmillan, 215–227.

Jensen, E. (2005). *Western Sahara: Anatomy of a Stalemate*. London: Lynne Rienner.

Jesseph, D. (1993). "Of Analytics and Indivisibles: Hobbes on the Methods of Modern Mathematics." *Revue d'histoire des sciences*, 46(2), 153–193.

Jung, O. (1995). *Plebizit und Diktatur. Die Abstimmungen der Nationalsozialisten*. Tubingen: Mohr.

Kaarsted, T. (1968). *Paskekrisen 1920*. Aarhus: Aarhus Universitetsforlag.

Kahn, E. (1960). "On the Road to Republic." *Annual Survey of South African Law*, 1, 1–2.

Karklins, R. (1994). *Ethnopolitics and Transition to Democracy. The Collapse of the USSR and Latvia*. Baltimore: Johns Hopkins University Press.

Karklins, R., and B. Zepa. (2001). "Political Participation in Latvia 1987–2001." *Journal of Baltic Studies*, 32(4), 334–346.

Kavanagh, D. (1996). *British Politics: Continuities and Change*. Oxford: Oxford University Press.

Kedourie, E. (1960). *Nationalism*. Oxford: Blackwell.

Kelsen, H. (1941). "The Pure Theory of Law and Analytical Jurisprudence." *Harvard Law Review*, 55(1), 44–70.

Key, J. (2008). "Foreign Policy Challenges Ahead." New Zealand Institute of International Affairs, Speech 8 April, 2008.

Key, V. O., Jr. (1968). *The Responsible Electorate: Rationality in Presidential Voting 1936–1960*. New York: Vintage Books.

Kirby, D. (1974). "Stockholm-Petrograd-Berlin: International Social Democracy and Finnish Independence." *Slavonic and East European Review*, 52(126), 63–84.

Kissane, B. (2012). "Is the Irish Referendum a Majoritarian Device?" In W. Marxer (ed.), *Direct Democracy and Minorities*. Heidelberg: Springer Verlag, 145–154.

Kissinger, H. (1957). *A World Restored: Metternich, Castlereagh and the Problems of Peace, 1812–22*. Boston: Houghton Mifflin.

———. (1994). *Diplomacy*. New York: Knopf.

Kitcher, P. (1982). *Abusing Science*. Cambridge, Mass.: MIT Press.

Klemperer, V. (1999). *I Shall Bear Witness: The Diaries of Victor Klemperer 1933–41*. London: Phoenix.

Krause, R. F. (2012). "Popular Votes and Independence for Montenegro." In W. Marxer (ed.). *Direct Democracy and Minorities*. Heidelberg: Springer Verlag, 22–30.

Laitin, D. (2002). "Comparative Politics: State of the Sub-Discipline." In I. Katznelson and H. V. Milner (eds.), *Political Science: The State of the Discipline*. New York: Norton, 630–659.

Lane, J. E., and S. Ersson. (2007). "Party System Instability in Europe: Persistent Differences in Volatility Between West and East?" *Democratisation*, 14(1), 92–110.

Laponce, J. (2001). "National Self-Determination and Referendums: The Case for Territorial Revisionism." *Nationalism and Ethnic Politics*, 7(2), 47–50.

———. (2010). *Le Référendum de souveraineté: Comparaisons, Critiques et Commentaires*. Québec: Les Presses de l'Université Laval.

Layne, C. (1994). "Kant or Cant: The Myth of the Democratic Peace." *International Security*, 19(2), 5–49.

LeDuc, L. (2003). *The Politics of Direct Democracy*. Toronto: Broadview Press.

Lee, E. C. (1981). "The American Experience 1778–1978." In A. Ranney (ed.), *The Referendum Device*. Washington, D.C.: AEI, 46–72.

Légaré, A. (1998). "An Assessment of Recent Political Development in Nunavut: The Challenges and Dilemmas of Inuit Self-Government." *Canadian Journal of Native Studies*, 18(2), 271–299.

Lijphart, A. (1977). *Democracy in Plural Societies: A Comparative Exploration*. New Haven, Conn.: Yale University Press.

———. (1984). *Democracies: Patterns of Majoritarian and Consensus Government in Twenty-One Countries*. New Haven, Conn.: Yale University Press.

———. (1999). *Patterns of Democracy: Government Forms and Performance in Thirty-Six Countries*. New Haven, Conn.: Yale University Press.

Lijphart, A., R. Rogowski, and K. Weaver. (1993). "Separation of Powers and Cleavage Management." In R. K. Weaver and B. A. Rockman (eds.), *Do Institutions Matter?*

Government Capabilities in the United States and Abroad. Washington, D.C.: Brookings Institution, 272–301.

Lindal, S. (2003). "Den Islandske Forfatningsprosessen." *Faroese Law Review*, 3(3), 184–196.

Linz, J. J. (1994). "Presidential or Parliamentary Government: Does It Make a Difference?" In J. J. Linz and A. Valenzuala (eds.), *The Failure of Presidential Government: Comparative Perspectives.* Baltimore: Johns Hopkins University Press, 3–90.

———. (2000). *Totalitarian and Authoritarian Regimes.* Boulder, Colo.: Lynne Rienner.

Lutz, G., and M. Marsh. (2007). "Introduction: Consequences of Low Turnout." *Electoral Studies*, 26(3), 539–547.

MacCormick, N. (2000). "Is There a Constitutional Path to Scottish Independence?" *Parliamentary Affairs*, 53, 725–726.

MacDonald, S. B. (1988). "Insurrection and Redemocratization in Suriname? The Ascendancy of the 'Third Path.'" *Journal of Interamerican Studies and World Affairs*, 30(1), 105–132.

Mac Ginty, R. (2003). "Constitutional Referendums and Ethnonational Conflict: The Case of Northern Ireland." *Nationalism and Ethnic Politics*, 9(2), 1–22.

Machado, K. G. (1978). "The Philippines in 1977: Beginning a 'Return to Normalcy'?" *Asian Survey*, 18(2), 202–211.

Machiavelli, N. (2002). "Exhortatio ad capessendam Italiam in libertatemque a barbaris vindicandam." In P. Alessandro Capata (ed.), *Machiavelli: Il Principe.* Rome: Newton, 95–98.

MacIntyre, S. (2004). *The Concise History of Australia.* Cambridge: Cambridge University Press.

Mack Smith, D. (1959). *Italy: A Modern History.* Ann Arbor: University of Michigan Press.

MacMillan, G. (2006). "The Referendum, the Courts and Representative Democracy in Ireland." *Political Studies*, 40(1), 67–78.

Madison, J. (1987). "Federalist 63." In J. Madison, J. Jay, and A. Hamilton, *The Federalist Papers.* London: Penguin, 369–375.

Magee, B. (2001). *The Story of Philosophy.* New York: DK Publishing.

Magleby, D. (1984). *Direct Legislation: Voting on Ballot Propositions in the United States.* Baltimore: Johns Hopkins University Press.

Maine, H. S. (1897). *Popular Government.* Indianapolis: Liberty Fund.

Mansergh, L. (1999). "Two Referendums and the Referendum Commission: The 1998 Experience." *Irish Political Studies*, 14(1), 123–131.

March, J., and J. P. Olsen. (1984). *Rediscovering Institutions.* New York: Free Press.

Maritain, J. (1961). *Man and the State.* Washington, D.C.: Catholic University of America Press.

Markakis, J. (1995). "Eritrea's National Charter." *Review of African Political Economy*, 22(63), 126–129.

Marsiliani, L., and T. Renström. (2007). "Political Institutions and Economic Growth." *Economics of Governance*, 8(3), 233–261.

Mattern, J. (1921). *The Employment of the Plebiscite in the Determination of Sovereignty.* Baltimore: Johns Hopkins University Press.

Mayer, K. B. (1968). "The Jura Problem: Ethnic Conflict in Switzerland." *Social Research*, 25, 707–741.

McAllister, I., and D. T. Studlar. (2000). "Conservative Euroscepticism and the Referendum Party in the 1997 British General Election." *Party Politics*, 6(3), 359–371.

McGarry, J., and B. O'Leary. (1993). "Introduction: The Macro-Political Regulation of Ethnic Conflict." In John McGarry and Brendan O'Leary (eds.), *The Politics of Ethnic Conflict Regulation: Case Studies of Protracted Ethnic Conflicts*. London: Routledge, 1–40, 204–467.

———. (1994). "The Political Regulation of National and Ethnic Conflict." *Parliamentary Affairs*, 47(1), 94–115.

———. (2006). "Consociational Theory, Northern Ireland's Conflict and Its Agreement. Part 1: What Consociationalists Can Learn from Northern Ireland?" *Government and Opposition*, 41(1), 43–63.

Medvedev, R. (1975). *On Socialist Democracy*. London: Macmillan.

Mill, J. S. (1890). *Considerations on Representative Government*. London: Holt.

———. (2008). "Considerations on Representative Government." In J. Gray (ed.), *John Stuart Mill: On Liberty and Other Essays*. Oxford: Oxford University Press, 205–470.

Miller, D. (1993). "In Defence of Rationality." *Journal of Applied Philosophy*, 10(1), 3–16.

Miller, M. (2004). "From Reform to Repression: The Post-New Order's Shifting Security Policies in Aceh." *Review of Indonesian and Malaysian Affairs*, 38(4), 129–162.

Mills, C. W. (1951). *The Sociological Imagination*. Oxford: Oxford University Press.

Ministerium für Bildung. (1997). *Lehrplan für die Sekundarstufe in der weiterführenden Schulen Hauptschule, Realschule, Gymnasium.* Kiel: Ministerium für Bildung des Landes Schleswig-Holstein (Hrsg.).

Mirow, M. C. (2004). "International Law and Religion in Latin America: The Beagle Channel Dispute." *Suffolk Transnational Law Review*, 28, 1–25.

Mitchell, J. (1992). "The Multi-Option Referendum: A Comparative Perspective." In A. McCartney (ed.), *Asking the People*. Edinburgh: Edinburgh University Press, 7–19.

Mitchell, P., G. Evans, and B. O'Leary. (2009). "Extremist Outbidding in Ethnic Party Systems Is Not Inevitable: Tribune Parties in Northern Ireland." *Political Studies*, 57(2), 397–421.

Möchli, S. (1994). *Direkte Demokratie*. Berne: Haupt.

Monnet, J. (1978). *Memoirs*. New York: Doubleday.

Morel, L. (1992). "Le référendum: Etat des recherches." *Revue Française de Science Politique*, 42(6), 835–864.

————. (1996). "Towards a Less Controversial Use of the Referendum in Europe." In M. Gallagher and P. Vincenzo Uleri (eds.), *The Referendum Experience in Europe*. Basingstoke: Macmillan, 66–85.

————. (2001). "The Strategic Use of Government-Sponsored Referendums in Liberal Democracies." In M. Mendelsohn and A. Parkin (eds.), *Referendum Democracy: Citizens, Elites, and Deliberation in Referendum Campaigns*. New York: Palgrave, 47–64.

————. (2005). "Le choix du référendum: Leçons françaises. L'émergence d'un référendum politiquement obligatoire." Paper presented at the ECPR General Conference, September 8–10, 2005, Budapest.

Mozart, W. A. (1791). *Die Zauberflöte*. Opera Journeys Libretto Series.

Munro, W. B. (1912). *The Initiative, The Referendum and the Recall*. New York: D. Appleton.

————. (1928). "Physics and Politics—An Old Analogy Revised." *American Political Science Review*, 23 (1), 1–11.

Nezavisimaya Gazeta. Editorial (1991, March 21). A1.

Nielsen, R. L. (2009). "The Logic of EU Referendums." Doctoral thesis, University of Southern Denmark.

————. (2012). "Det Dumme Folk." In R. L. Nielsen (ed.), *40 år siden danskerne stemte ja til Europa*. Copenhagen: Magasinet Europa, 45–50.

Nohlen, D., M. Krennerich, and B. Thibaut. (1999). *Elections in Africa: A Data Handbook*. Oxford: Oxford University Press.

Noorani, A. G. (2001). "Review Article: Jinnah and Junagadh." *Frontline*, 18(21), 13–26.

Nordlund, K. (1905). *The Swedish-Norwegian Union Crisis: A History with Documents*. Wiksell, Upsala.

North, D. C. (1991). "Institutions." *Journal of Economic Perspectives*, 5(1), 97–104.

Nurmi, H. (1997). "Referendum Design: An Exercise in Applied Social Choice Theory." *Scandinavian Political Studies*, 20(1), 33–52.

Oakeshott, M. (1991). *Rationalism in Politics and Other Essays*. Indianapolis: Liberty Fund.

Oklopcic, Z. (2012). "Independence Referendums and Democratic Theory in Quebec and Montenegro." *Nationalism and Ethnic Politics*, 18(1), 22–42.

O'Leary, B. (2001a). "The Elements of Right-Sizing and Right-Peopling the State." In B. O'Leary, I. S. Lustick, and T. Callaghy (eds.), *Right-Sizing the State: The Politics of Moving Borders*. Oxford: Oxford University Press, 15–73.

————. (2001b). "Introduction." In B. O'Leary, I. S. Lustick, and T. Callaghy (eds.), *Right-Sizing the State: The Politics of Moving Borders*. Oxford: Oxford University Press, 1–14.

O'Leary, B., I. S. Lustick, and T. Callaghy (eds.). (2001). *Right-Sizing the State: The Politics of Moving Borders*. Oxford: Oxford University Press.

O'Mahony, J. (2009). "Ireland's EU Referendum Experience." *Irish Political Studies*, 24(4), 429–444.

Ortega y Gasset, J. (1937). *La rebellión de las massas.* Madrid: Colección Austral.

Orwell, G. (1953). "Notes on Nationalism." In Sonia Orwell and Ian Angus (Editors) *The Penguin Essays of George Orwell*, London: Penguin, 306–323.

Osborne, R. (1982). "Voting Behaviour in Northern Ireland 1921–1977." In F. Boal and J. Douglas (eds.), *Integration and Division: Geographical Perspectives on the Northern Ireland Problem.* London: Academic Press, 137–166.

Pavkovic, A., and P. Radan. (2007). *Creating New States: Theory and Practice of Secession.* Aldershot: Ashgate.

Pedersen, M. N. (1979). "The Dynamics of European Party Systems: Changing Patterns of Electoral Volatility." *European Journal of Political Research*, 7(1), 1–26.

Peretz, D. (1959). "Democracy and Revolution in Egypt." *Middle East Journal*, 13(1), 26–40.

Petersen, N. (1975). *Folket og udenrigspolitikken: Med særligt henblik på Danmarks forhold til EF.* Copenhagen: Gyldendal.

Pierce, R., H. Valen, and O. Listhaug. (1983). "Referendum Voting Behavior: The Norwegian and British Referenda on Membership in the European Community." *American Journal of Political Science*, 27, 43–63.

Pinelli, C. (2006). "The 1948 Italian Constitution and the 2006 Referendum: Food for Thought." *European Constitutional Law Review*, 2(3), 329–340.

Popper, K. (1959). *Logic of Scientific Discovery.* London: Routledge and Kegan Paul.

———. (1963). *Conjectures and Refutations: The Growth of Scientific Knowledge.* London: Routledge and Kegan Paul.

Przeworski, A. (2007). "Is the Science of Comparative Politics Possible?" In S. Stokes and C. Boix (eds.), *The Oxford Handbook of Comparative Politics.* Oxford: Oxford University Press, 147–171.

Québec Ministry of State for Electoral and Parliamentary Reform. (1977). "Consulting the People of Québec."

Quine, W. W. O. (1951). "Two Dogmas of Empiricism." *Philosophical Review*, 60(1), 20–43.

Qvortrup, M. (1999). "A. V. Dicey: The Referendum as the People's Veto." *History of Political Thought*, 20(3), 531–546.

———. (2000). "Israel's Supermajority." Working paper, Initiative and Referendum Institute, www.iandrinstitute.org.

———. (2001a). "How to Lose a Referendum." *Political Quarterly*, 72(2), 90–100.

———. (2001b). "Regulation of Direct Democracy Outside the USA: Impressions, Tendencies and Patterns from Overseas." In M. Dane Waters (ed.), *The Battle over Citizen Lawmaking.* Durham, N.C.: Carolina Academic Press, 239–250.

———. (2002). *A Comparative Study of Referendums: Government by the People.* Manchester: Manchester University Press.

————. (2003). *The Political Philosophy of Jean-Jacques Rousseau: The Impossibility of Reason.* Manchester: Manchester University Press.

————. (2006). "Democracy by Delegation: The Decision to Hold Referendums in the United Kingdom." *Representation*, 42(1), 59–72.

————. (2012). "The History of Ethno-National Referendums." *Nationalism and Ethnic Politics*, 18(1), 139–150.

Radan, P. (2000). "Post-Secession International Borders: A Critical Analysis of the Opinions of Badinter." *Melbourne Law Review*, 50(1), 50–75.

————. (2006). "Indestructible Union. of Indestructible States: The Supreme Court of the United States and Secession." *Legal History*, 10, 187–207.

Räikkönen, E. (1938). *Svinhufvud, the Builder of Finland: An Adventure in Statecraft.* Helsinki: A. Wilmer.

Ranney, A. (1981). "Regulating the Referendum." In A. Ranney (ed.), *The Referendum Device*. Washington, D.C.: American Enterprise Institute, 89–112.

Reilly, B. (2003). "Democratic Validation." In J. Darby and R. Mac Ginty (eds.), *Contemporary Peace Making*. London: Palgrave Macmillan, 175–189.

Rein, A. (2000). *Borderland: A Journey Through the History of the Ukraine.* Boulder, Colo.: Westview.

Remington, T. F. (2006). "Politics in Russia." In G. Almond, K. Stroem, R. Dalton, and G. B. Powell (eds.), *Comparative Politics Today: A World View*. New York: Pearson, 364–410.

Renan, E. (1992). *Qu'est-ce qu'une nation? et autres essais politiques.* Paris: Presses Pocket.

Riker, W. (1975). "Federalism." In F. Greenstein and N. Polsby (eds.), *Governmental Institutions and Processes. Handbook of Political Science*. Vol. 5. Reading, Mass.: Addison-Wesley, 93–172.

Roberts, S. (2007, May 17). "New Demographic Racial Gap Emerges." *New York Times*, A1.

Rocard, M. (1988). "Discours de M. Michel Rocard, Premier ministre, sur les accords de Matignon et l'avenir de la Nouvelle-Calédonie et sur la nécessité de voter oui au référendum du 6 novembre, à Belfort le 25 octobre et à Rennes le 27 octobre 1988." http://discours.vie-publique.fr/notices/883386300.html (accessed January 8, 2012).

Rokkan, S. (1970). *Citizens, Elections and Parties.* Oslo: Universitetsforlaget.

Ross, M. L. (2005). *Understanding Civil War.* Washington, D.C.: World Bank Group.

Rouke, J. T., P. Hiskes, and C. E. Zirakzadeh. (1992). *Direct Democracy and International Politics: Deciding International Issues Through Referendums.* Oxford: Lynne Rienner.

Rousseau, J.-J. (1993). "Du Contrat Social." In *Œuvres III*. Paris: Gallimard, 351–470.

Ruin, O. (1996). "Sweden: The Referendum as an Instrument for Defusing Political Issues." In M. Gallagher and P. Vincenzo Uleri (eds.), *The Referendum Experience in Europe*. Basingstoke: Macmillan, 171–184.

Schedler, A. (2006). *Electoral Authoritarianism: The Dynamics of Unfree Competition.* Boulder, Colo.: Lynne Rienner.

Schmemann, S. (1991). "Soviet Vote Becomes Test of Loyalties." *New York Times,* 28 March, A1.

Schmidt, E. (2009). "Anticolonial Nationalism in French West Africa: Made Guinea Unique?" *African Studies Review,* 52(2), 1–34.

Schmitt, C. (1926). *Volksentscheid und Volksbegehren. Ein Beitrag zur Auslegung der Weimarer Verfassung und zur Lehre von der unmittelbaren Demokratie.* Berlin: Walter de Gruyter.

———. (1932). *Legalität und Legitimität.* Berlin: Duncker & Humblot.

———. (1934). "Der Führer schützt des Rechts: Zur Reichstagsrede Adolf Hitlers vom 13. Juli 1934." *Deutsche Juristen-Zeitung,* 39(15), 945–950.

———. (1936). "Die Deutsche Rechtswissenschaft in der Kampf gegen den jüdischen Geist." *Deutsche Juristenzeitung,* 41(20), 1193–1194.

———. (1985). *The Crisis of Parliamentary Democracy.* E. Kennedy (trans.). Cambridge, Mass.: MIT Press.

Schulze, K. E. (2001). "The East Timor Referendum Crisis and Its Impact on Indonesian Politics." *Studies in Conflict and Terrorism,* 24(1), 77–82.

Schumacher, W. (1932). "Thirty Years of the People's Rule in Oregon." *Political Science Quarterly,* 46, 242–258.

Schumpeter, J. (1942). *Capitalism, Socialism and Democracy.* London: Routledge.

Scruton, R. (1995). *A Short History of Modern Philosophy.* London: Routledge.

Secretary-General, SG/SM/11568, GA/COL/3171.

Setälä, M. L. (1999). *Referendums and Democratic Government: Normative Theory and the Analysis of Institutions.* Basingstoke: Macmillan.

Seyd, B. (1998). "Regulating the Referendum." *Representation,* 35(4), 191–199.

Sheehy, A. (1991, March). "The All-Union and RSFSR Referendums of March 17." *Report on the USSR,* 19–23.

Sølvará, H. A. (2003). "Færøernes Statsretlige Stilling i Historisk Belysning—Mellem selvstyre og Selvbestemmelse." *Faroese Law Review,* 3(3), 145– 182.

———. (2010, September). "90 ár síðan føroyingar vrakaðu Grundlógina." *Dimmalætting,* 27–28.

Spiermann, O. (1998). "Hvad kommer efter tyve- en analyse af Højesterets dom i grundlovssagen." *Ugeskrift for Retsvæsen (UFR),* 131, 325–335.

Suksi, M. (1994). *Bringing in the People: A Comparison of the Constitutional Forms and Practices of the Referendum.* Dordrecht: Kluwer.

———. (2003). "Sub-state Solutions as Expressions of Self-Determination." *Faroese Law Review,* 3(3), 197–230.

Sussman, G. (2006). "The Referendum as an Electoral Device in National Party Politics, 1917–60." *Politikon, South African Journal of Political Studies,* 33(3), 259–275.

Szczerbiak, A., and P. Taggart. (2004). "The Politics of European Referendum Outcomes and Turnout: Two Models." *West European Politics,* 27(4), 557–583.

Talaska, R. A. (1988). "Analytic and Synthetic Method According to Hobbes." *Journal of the History of Philosophy*, 26(2), 207–237.

Tarr, A. G. (1997). "New Judicial Federalism in Perspective." *Notre Dame Law Review*, 72, 1097–1131.

Terret, J. (2000). *The Dissolution of Yugoslavia and the Badinter Arbitration*. Princeton, N.J.: Princeton University Press.

Thorsteinson, J., and S. Rasmussen. (1999). "Rigsfællesskabet mellem Danmark og Færøerne." In O. S. Andersen (ed.), *Folketingest Festskrift i anledning af Grundlovens 150 års jubilæum den 5. Juni 1999*. Copenhagen: Folketinget, 491–532.

Tierney, S. (2012). *Constitutional Referendums: The Theory and Practice of Republican Deliberation*. Oxford: Oxford University Press.

Tsebelis, G. (1990). *Nested Games: Rational Choice in Comparative Politics*. Berkeley: University of California Press.

———. (2002). *Veto Players: How Political Institutions Work*. Princeton, N.J.: Princeton University Press.

United Nations. (1956). "Report of the Plebiscite Administrator on the Plebiscite Held in Togoland Under the British Administration on 9 May 1956" (T/1269).

———. (1993, August 11). "United Nations Observer Mission to Verify the Referendum in Eritrea: Report of the Secretary-General."

Vedung, E. (2007). *Unionsdebatten 1905: En jämförelse mellan argumenteringen i Sverige och Norge*. Unpublished doctoral dissertation, Uppsala University.

Vienna Commission. (2002). "Code of Good Practice in Electoral Matters: Guidelines and Explanatory Report—Adopted by the Venice Commission at its 52nd session (Venice, 18–19 October 2002" (CDL-AD(2002)023rev).

von Martens, G. F. (1801). *Recueil de principaux traits d'alliance de paix*. Göttingen: J. C. Dieterich.

Walker, E. W. (2003). *Dissolution: Sovereignty and the Breakup of the USSR*. Boulder, Colo.: Rowman & Littlefield.

Walton, D. N. (1991). "Bias, Critical Doubt, and Fallacies." *Argumentation and Advocacy*, 1–28.

Wambaugh, S. (1933). *Plebiscites Since the World War*. Washington, D.C.: Carnegie Endowment for International Peace.

Ward, A. W., and G. P. Gooch. (1923). *The Cambridge History of British Foreign Policy 1783–1919*. Cambridge: Cambridge University Press.

Watts, R. (1999). "Processes of Constitutional Restructuring: The Canadian Experience in Comparative Context." Working paper 1, Queens University.

Webber, J. (1996). "Legality of a Unilateral Declaration of Independence Under Canadian Law." *McGill Law Journal*, 42, 281–309.

Weber, M. (1978). *Economy and Society*. G. Roth and C. Wittich (eds.). Berkeley: University of California Press.

Wheatley, J. (2012). "The Disruptive Potential of Direct Democracy in Deeply Divided Societies." In W. Marxer (ed.), *Direct Democracy and Minorities*. Heidelberg: Springer Verlag, 64–73.

Whelan, A. (1994). "Wilsonian Self-Determination and the Versailles Settlement." *International and Comparative Law Quarterly*, 43(1), 99–115.

White, S., and R. J. Hill. (1996). "Russia, the former Soviet Union and Eastern Europe: the referendum as a flexible political instrument." In M. Gallagher and P.V. Uleri (eds.), *The Referendum Experience in Europe*. Basingstoke: Macmillan, 153-170.

Wildavsky, A. (1973). "If Planning Is Everything—Maybe It's Nothing." *Policy Sciences*, 4(2), 127–153.

Williams, G., and D. Hume. (2010). *People Power: The History and Future of the Referendum in Australia*. Sydney: University of New South Wales Press.

Wirth, L. (1936). "Types of Nationalism." *American Journal of Sociology*, 41(6), 723–737.

Wirtschaft und Statistik. (1934). "Die Volksabstimmung über das Staatsoberhaupt des deutschen Reichs am 19. August 1934." *Wirtschaft und Statistik*, 14 (January–June), 552–553.

Wolchik, S. L. (1995). "The Politics of Transition and the Break-up of Czechoslovakia." In J. Musil (ed.), *The End of Czechoslovakia*. Budapest: Central European University Press, 225–244.

Wooster, R. A. (1961). "The Secession of the Lower South: An Examination of Changing Interpretations." *Civil War History*, 7(2), 117–127.

Wyller, T. C. (1992). *Skal Folket Bestemme? Folkeavstemning som Politisk Prosess*. Oslo: Univrsitetsforlaget.

Wyn Jones, R., and R. Scully. (2012). *Wales Says Yes: Devolution and the 2011 Welsh Referendum*. Cardiff: University of Wales Press.

Zurcher, A. J. (1935). "The Hitler Referenda." *American Political Science Review*, 29(1), 91–99.

Index

A c k n o w l e d g m e n t s

This book began on the back on an envelope on a UN chartered plane from Juba to Khartoum in the Sudan. I am indebted to Brendan O'Leary, my travel companion on the aforementioned journey, for suggesting that I write this book and for his wise counsel during all stages. I am also indebted to my editors at University of Pennsylvania Press, Peter Agree and Julia Roberts. I am also grateful for help and suggestions from scholars and practitioners, including Sir David Butler, Arend Lijphart, Sir Derek Plumley, Hans Andrias Sølvará, Rein Taagepera, Beogang He, Maija Setälä, Markku Suksi, Josep Colomer, Bjørn Erik Rasch, Dahlia Scheindlin, Peter Radan, Chris Chapman, Jean Laponce, and to Nina Bamford for research assistance. I am grateful for their comments and suggestions, but bear sole responsibility for inevitable shortcomings of this work. I am also grateful to my sons Fred and Sebastian for distracting me. This book is dedicated to Anne for her love and patience.